The Likeability Trap

The Likeability Trap

HOW TO BREAK FREE AND SUCCEED AS YOU ARE

Alicia Menendez

HARPER
BUSINESS

An Imprint of HarperCollinsPublishers

FIRST EDITION

Photograph by Africa Studio/Shutterstock, Inc.

Library of Congress Cataloging-in-Publication Data has been applied for.

ISBN 978-0-06-283876-6

19 20 21 22 23 LSC 10 9 8 7 6 5 4 3 2 1

For Jane, who is always herself

To be nobody-but-yourself—in a world which is doing its best, night and day, to make you everybody else—means to fight the hardest battle which any human being can fight; and never stop fighting.

—*e. e. cummings*

Contents

Part I

Please Like Me

I have to admit something to you, something I hate to admit: it is very important to me that you like me. This has always been the case, and it has taken many forms, including, but not limited to: gratuitous smiling, rapid response time, holding my tongue, changing the way I look, pretending not to care (but still caring), and judging myself for caring, to name a few.

I had always assumed that the degree to which I cared was unique to me. In 2015, I learned that I was wrong.

That year I traveled to Albuquerque, New Mexico, to give a speech in front of six hundred professional women at a conference hosted by the American Business Women's Association. While on one hand I am "all business," in reality I know little about *actual* business, so I instead used the speech as a personal therapy session. At the time, I was anchoring a television show on a third-tier cable network. I was struggling with constant and competing feedback about who I should be, everything from how I styled my hair ("her forehead is too big for a center part") to how I, an old soul, communicated my youth (more T-shirts) to how I navigated the internal politics of an office that was part media company, part start-up, part grand experiment (lots of crying in bathroom stalls). With all of this incoming, unsolicited, and often contradictory commentary, I was slowly coming to terms with the fact that I might not be able to make everyone happy, and that in order to do what was necessary to ensure my and my team's success, I might need to ruffle some feathers.

Around the same time, Chimamanda Ngozi Adichie, the writer and MacArthur Grant genius whose TED Talk was used on the track for Beyoncé's song "Flawless," told an audience that likeability is "bullshit." Adichie's proclamation set the internet ablaze and made me wonder if the fact that I largely valued my own worth by my likeability meant that I myself was bullshit. Was my caring—as a Cancer, a cryer, an INFJ (Introvert, Intuitive, Feeling, Judging)—holding me back? I wanted to be myself, do good work, lead my team, and feel, well, liked. Why did that seem so hard?

In my gut, I knew I wasn't alone in caring, even if I cared more than most. Some light internet research confirmed that women face a likeability penalty in everything from hiring to promotions. I knew that women running for office have to prove that they are likeable *and* competent. Plus, as women, we're taught to care about what others think of us. I couldn't possibly be the only one who made it to adulthood without shaking that mandate, could I?

On that stage in Albuquerque, I looked out at the crowd of women, grabbed the sides of the podium with sweaty palms, and hoped for the best. I shared with the audience my own desire to be well liked, and the many times that ran into conflict with my efforts to lead. I explored the contradictory messages of the importance of likeability and the importance of authenticity. I then suggested that perhaps attendees use this conference to try "caring less" on for size. Who would they be if they took a few days to just be themselves?

When I finished giving my speech, the crowd didn't cheer; they *roared*. When the host of the event opened the floor up for questions, women streamed to two microphone stands at the front of the room. Most of them didn't have questions; they had *testimonials*.

Their peers saw them as nice ladies, but not leadership material. They spoke in every meeting and advocated on behalf of their teams, and then got reviews suggesting that they round off their edges. They wanted to get ahead, but they wanted to get ahead as themselves.

I had struck a nerve.

At the end of these statements, their voices inflected upward, and their hands flew into the air, intimating a question. Those queries were, in essence, always the same: *If likeability matters, but I can't be both likeable and successful, then where does that leave me? If I need to act one way to be seen as a leader, but acting that way makes me less likeable and that performance makes me less authentic, then is it really working? And how do I learn to care less when I keep being told that I should care more?*

I wasn't alone in feeling what I was feeling. I had uncovered an unspoken frustration. Now I needed to figure out what to do about it.

First, I needed to be sure that these six hundred women from across the country weren't outliers or fakers who were just trying to make me feel better about being a thirty-something who couldn't seem to get a grip. I started by asking my friends, and their friends, if it was important to them to be well liked. I found that many of them felt the same way I did; they care deeply about being liked by friends, by colleagues, and by supervisors. "This is the story of my life!" multiple women exclaimed. Many women were ashamed of how much they cared, deeming it "superficial" or "pathetic." Others wore it as a badge of honor; they celebrated their likeability as an ability to tap into others' feelings and needs.

Many of the women who admitted to caring about likeability were surprised to learn that there are people in the world for whom being well liked isn't a priority, or women who don't spend their days attempting to please others. Sometimes they were envious of those non-carers; sometimes they were judgmental. One woman described people who don't care about being liked as "probably on the scale of psychotic."

But it turns out, those women do exist! Women who are genuinely unfazed by what others think of them, women who looked at me blankly when I described my personal obsession. My own mother was puzzled by how much I cared whether or not others liked me. "I assume everyone likes me," she said self-confidently. "And if they don't? Well, screw them."

Their explanations for why they didn't care or couldn't care varied. Some women credited their parents for cultivating a sense of self that seemed impenetrable by others; others had taught themselves to care less. "The work should speak for itself," was one rationale. "It's more important to me to be respected than to be well liked" was a common refrain, especially from more seasoned professionals. Some, particularly women of color, deemed likeability a luxury they could not afford or were disinterested in.

As someone who was motivated by likeability, I imagined

women who don't care about likeability to all be living their best lives, being their authentic selves at work and at home. Marching to the beat of their own drummer! Dancing like no one was watching! Cutting loose those friends who were inconsiderate or judgmental, challenging those bosses who demanded conformity. But it turns out that even those who have a very clear and fixed internal compass independent of others' perceptions acknowledged that they had, at points, paid a price for being so brazenly themselves. Many of them conceded that they had been penalized for not playing office politics or for not pretending to be perpetually pleasant. Some even admitted that it had limited their career advancement. One woman offered me this important distinction: although she is not motivated by likeability, it doesn't hurt any less when someone expresses their distaste for her.

Speaking with these women, thinking critically about my own professional journey, and reading the existing research on women and likeability, I realized that whether you care or you don't care what others think of you, there are still traps all around that will be an obstacle to getting ahead.

TRAP 1: THE GOLDILOCKS CONUNDRUM. OR, SHE'S TOO WARM; SHE'S TOO STRONG; SHE'S RARELY JUST RIGHT.

A warm woman is well liked, but the workplace, especially in male-dominated fields, often values something different: strength. That means that a woman who starts out friendly, nurturing, and sweet—regardless of her actual competence—will often be told that she doesn't have what it takes to lead. She'll be coached to be stronger and more assertive. She will be counseled to lower her voice and drape her arms over the back of her chair to take up more space in meetings. On the other hand, the woman who starts out strong—who asks for what she wants, advocates on behalf of herself and her team, and demonstrates comfort with confrontation—will be told that she is too much. Too pushy. Too demanding. Too aggressive. This Goldilocks Conundrum is further complicated by other cultural markers such as race, ethnicity, sexual orientation, and parenthood.

For a woman who is naturally warm, the attempt to appear strong has a strange side effect: it can make her less likeable. For a woman who is naturally strong, the attempt to appear warm will be additionally confusing as she watches her male peers be lauded for the very things she is cautioned against.

TRAP 2: LIKEABILITY AND AUTHENTICITY AS LUXURIES. OR, NOT EVERYONE GETS TO BE THEMSELVES AT WORK.

If authenticity is necessary to be likeable, and critical to effective leadership, but women are encouraged to spend most of their careers trying to be more of whatever it is they're told they're not, how can they possibly be authentic, likeable, and effective leaders? In penalizing strong women for not being warm enough, and in punishing warm women for not being strong enough, are we telling women that there is no way for them to lead as themselves?

And what does authenticity mean for those who are minorities in their industry or workplace? Is being your authentic self and being well liked a luxury afforded to everyone or only to those who align with the dominant office culture?

TRAP 3: DAMNED IF YOU DO. OR, THE ROAD TO SUCCESS IS LINED WITH EVEN MORE TRAPS.

Likeability, we are told, is integral to success. But ambitious women know, and the research supports the notion that the more successful a woman becomes, the less others like her.

In addition to ability and hard work, the very things one needs to do in order to advance in most careers often involve advocating for one's ideas, one's self, and one's accomplishments. Each of the necessary skills that entails—asking for a promotion or a raise, negotiating a salary, taking credit for a job well done—makes women less likeable. It's not just craving success or finding success that makes women less likeable; the most basic actions necessary to succeed (or just, like, pay your bills) make women seem less likeable. At every turn, it feels as though women are being asked to choose between success and likeability.

At the same time, the higher a successful woman rises, the more likely others are to be suspicious of her, to doubt her motives, and to assume that she is cold and unlikeable. "She succeeded, and for a woman, that is so rare," the thinking goes. "She must have been willing to do anything to get there."

The "success penalty," as this phenomenon is often referred to, is made worse because so many ambitious women, women like myself, feel we were raised to value two things: success *and* likeability, only to learn the hard way that they might be mutually exclusive. For us, the success penalty isn't merely a professional impediment; it's a mindfuck. It threatens not just our upward mobility but our very sense of self.

All of these traps ask women to dedicate significant mind share to supposed deficiencies. What if, instead, that time and energy could be rededicated to things such as hard skills, building contacts, or, I don't know, sleeping? What would happen if we let women lead as they are?

The constant chatter about *how* women do their work and *how* women lead makes it nearly impossible for women to lead in a way that is authentic to them. Rather than reimagining leadership, we're asking women to reimagine themselves. That is robbing all of us of the opportunity to create a model of leadership that is more expansive, includes more of us, and yields better results.

EVEN IF LIKEABILITY DOESN'T MATTER, THESE TRAPS DO

Here is the good news: you are not alone! If it feels hard to navigate these questions of what it means to be a woman, to lead and to be liked as you, it's because it is! (And if you feel like I am using a lot of exclamation points to not allow you to fall into a funk, it's because I am!!!!) Acknowledging that balancing authenticity, likeability, and the quest for leadership might be elusive, if not impossible, while frustrating at first, can be liberating. You're probably not doing it wrong; the system is set up so that it is nearly impossible to do it right.

This is particularly true because we are in a period of profound change. The #MeToo movement has spurred a widespread cultural reckoning. We are not only questioning those in power; we are questioning the systems of power that have fostered environments of harassment and abuse.

But even as the winds of change nip at our neck and the ground beneath us shifts, how to self-present, especially at work, can actually seem *more* confusing. Are we playing by the old rules or the new rules? The old rules didn't apply to all of us; do the new rules? Who is writing the new rules and how do we get a seat at the drafting table? Speaking up and out has brought many women reconciliation, but for many it has also come at a price. Often the public narrative is different from what is whispered behind closed doors. A woman who speaks out against injustice can be seen as both a hero in the world and a problem in her industry. How does this change really take hold? Many of us walk into a workplace every day where it is hard to know if the higher-ups are busy rewriting the organization's sexual harassment policy to cover their ass, or if they are really grappling with the underlying assumptions about who is worthy of agency and power.

When it comes to women and work, there are issues that may feel more urgent than likeability, including a gender wage gap (one that is particularly dramatic for women of color), and the culture of sexual harassment that #MeToo is exposing in every industry from entertainment and politics to farm work and domestic services. Although women continue to reach higher levels of educational and professional attainment, we're continually reminded that there is still a big power gap waiting to be filled.

That gap is most stark at the leadership tier. Women constitute slightly more than half of the U.S. population, yet we make up less than 25 percent of the U.S. Congress, and hold less than 23 percent of the seats on corporate boards for Fortune 500 companies. Among the directors of the 100 top-grossing movies of 2017, fewer were women than were men named James and Michael. For women of color, that gap is even wider. Minority women account for about 18 percent of the entire U.S. population, yet fewer than 1 percent of Fortune 500 companies have those women at the helm. Notably, the 116th Congress boasts a record number of women of color but, at 11 percent, it is still short of proportional representation.

Research affirms that the leading obstacles to women's leadership are stereotypes and bias. The thing that feels the most amorphous and the least correctable is also the most pernicious. Among the biases women face: the double bind between likeability and success, and the paradoxical calls for gender-correcting performance and authenticity in a woman leader.

The constant trade-offs between competence and likeability

have real consequences. These perceptions can affect hiring, negotiations, and career advancement. Some women, those nearing the top, may take on the terrifying glass cliff, assuming that a high-risk, high-reward situation is their only shot at clearing the likeability-competence hurdle. And plenty of women, sensing that they cannot win in a male-dominated industry, opt out and pursue careers in industries that are gender-diverse or mostly women. That can be necessary and rewarding for the individual, but if women keep opting out of the game because the game is rigged, are we forever conceding the realms of math, science, tech, business, politics, and so much more to men? And beyond the consequences at work, there are consequences for the women themselves. In trying to be everything all at once, women are straight-up exhausted.

LIKEABILITY IS IN THE EYE OF THE BEHOLDER

So, what *is* likeability exactly? Is likeability about being pleasant? Friendly? Agreeable? Charming? There are friendly people who aren't likeable. There are agreeable people who are frustrating in their lack of conviction. There are charming people whom you just can't trust.

One's personality is composed, at its core, of five basic traits. Experts in psychology call them the "Big Five," easily remembered for dinner-party reference by the acronym OCEAN: Openness to experience, Conscientiousness, Extroversion, Agreeableness, and Neuroticism. In the context of the Big Five, "Openness to experience" can take various forms: intellectual curiosity, creativity, and a belief that variety, not sriracha, is the spice of life. Conscientiousness is an ability to control one's impulses, and to channel one's energy toward a goal. Extroversion is about how much energy a person derives from social situations. Are you recharged after a big party? Or do you slink away, needing a nap? Agreeableness is defined by how well you get along with others. Neuroticism is about confidence and comfort (or discomfort) with one's self.

All of these traits exist on a sliding scale. My mother would say she's "open to experience" and, by many measures, she is. She went to college out of state, married someone outside of her own ethnic group at a time when that was a progressive thing to do, and she loves to travel. On the other hand, when you ask her what she'd like to order for dinner, she'll say, "You know me. I'm easy. Anything except sushi, Mexican, Indian, Thai, or Vietnamese. Actually, why don't we just get pizza?" I am an undercover introvert—I have the capacity to be chatty and sociable, but I'm happiest when someone I have plans with cancels them (preferably via text), leaving me to put on a nice pair of sweatpants and fall asleep on the couch.

By forming the basis of our personalities, these traits also contribute to our likeability. Studies have found a correlation between people who are extroverted and agreeable, and measures of likeability. Neuroticism is the one trait of the Big Five that brings with it a pretty consistent likeability demerit. (People who are uncomfortable with themselves have a tendency to make others feel the same in their presence.) But even the Big Five don't totally land on any one truth about likeability.

Likeability is often confused with popularity, but that's not exactly right, either. You can be well liked and not be popular. You can be popular and not be well liked. Popularity is about status; likeability is about how people actually feel about you.

As nebulous as it is, likeability can make or break a brand's reputation or an individual's performance review. It is critical to building relationships that allow you to rely on others for introductions and favors. In a group, likeability is key to establishing influence. In politics, voters overwhelmingly say it is important that they like a candidate they support. In daily life, the degree to which we're liked can impact our appeal as a friend and a mate.

Or, if you're like me, you just enjoy the validation that comes from knowing that other people like you, that your Instagram posts get likes, and that you have a five-star Lyft rating. You see, beyond the utility of likeability, there is a certain validation that comes from being well liked, especially when you are well liked for being you.

To be seen, and known, and then liked for being that person, creates psychological safety and comfort. In those environments where others can say, "We see you, and we get you," we feel empowered to thrive. We trust ourselves to be more creative, and to take bigger risks. Where it is absent, we are more likely to doubt ourselves.

Given the stakes, there is limitless content dedicated to helping you become a more likeable version of yourself. First published in 1936, Dale Carnegie's *How to Win Friends and Influence People* cemented his place as the father of self-help. His principles of human interaction are straightforward and widely applicable. Don't criticize or condemn others. Don't complain. Express appreciation. Consider others' motivations. One part of his book, "Six Ways to Make People Like You," includes principles such as cultivating a genuine interest in other people. Smiling. Using people's names. Encouraging others to talk about themselves. Listening. Talking in terms of others' interests. Making other people feel important. You'd think that only sociopaths need this type of advice, but it turns out we all do. (Side note: a few years ago I tweeted that one of my peers, a manager, needed to read Carnegie's book, and the Dale Carnegie Institute sent me two free copies! Consider this the seventh way to make people like you: send them free stuff.)

Carnegie's book has sold 30 million copies worldwide, because if you can execute these skills with sincerity, it's all decent advice. Most people love to talk about themselves! Most people love to hear their own names! Most people love to be treated like people! These are all great ways to improve one's likeability and become a more thoughtful person. Carnegie's book and many of the books that followed in his footsteps are useful. Feel free to casually drop one on the desk of whomever in your office doesn't practice the basic rules of kindness and civility, or who keeps calling you Karen even though your name is Kim.

My issue with guides to likeability is not the guides themselves; it is the misinterpretation of them. If you're like me, you might have walked away from those well-intended books thinking that it meant you could control whether or not other people like you. You can't. You can't make people like you, because that's just not how people or likeability works.

There are elements of how you interact with others that you can control. You can be kind, curious, and friendly. But how someone will interpret those qualities is out of your control.

It's hard to answer the question "What is likeability?" because behind how agreeable we find someone or how much we are drawn to them, what it is about them that creates our perception of them is wildly subjective. Research on the Big Five suggests that neuroticism makes people less likeable, but I for one enjoy a person who has just enough neurotic tendencies! (Someone who overapologizes, returns compliments and well-wishes even when they don't make sense [telling a flight attendant you hope *they* have a great trip], or starts to sweat anytime a text ellipse lasts a beat too long: I love you all!). You can execute all the likeability advice, sincerely, and still have others find you unlikeable. Because let's be honest, Reader: if likeability were as simple as using people's names, Reader, wouldn't we all just train ourselves to be likeable, Reader?

Likeability is more complex than any one agreed-upon set of qualities or learned behaviors. I like sensitive, high self-disclosers who are discerning about other people, slightly neurotic, and tell great stories. Extra points for those who constantly contradict themselves by doing things like talking about living a gluten-free life while eating a bread basket or saving the environment while ordering off Amazon Prime. They delight me! Those are my people; they may not be for everyone.

LIKEABILITY AS SOCIALLY ACCEPTABLE BIAS

In addition to being challenging to define, the biases that underlie likeability are hard to call out. Our notions of what makes a likeable person are riddled with deeply ingrained cultural biases, often based on gender, race, and ethnicity. Some of this bias may be explicit attitudes, positive and negative, we *consciously* hold about others. But most of this bias is subconscious, and even those of us who pride ourselves on being objective rely on some basic beliefs about individuals and groups to form quick assessments.

Women are expected to be warm and communal. Many people may not *consciously* hold that belief about women, yet when women violate that expectation of warmth and communality, others instinctively find them less likeable. For women who strive to lead, we need to be well liked in order to succeed, but we also become less likeable the more we succeed. For women of color, this comes with an extra degree of complexity—because we are supposed to comply with what is expected of us not only based on gender, but also based on our race and ethnicity. For Latinas like myself, we're either humble or we're hot-blooded. Asian-American women are actually penalized for the perception of being "unfairly competent."

For black women, being assertive is read as being aggressive. Add additional markers of identity—queerness, a disability, motherhood—and the invisible scorecard on which you are measured adjusts yet again.

If bias is one of the biggest barriers to women's advancement, and likeability is critical to that advancement, but influenced by bias, is it possible that likeability is sometimes used as a cover to express bias? How often is saying "I just don't like her" or "He's not a good fit" one of the last socially acceptable ways to say, "I'd rather vote for a man," "I'd prefer to hire someone white," or "I'm uncomfortable with gay people"? Are employers allowed to hide behind the subjective cloak of who they like and who they don't, who "fits" and who does not, as a not-so-subtle expression of bias?

Hiding behind likeability as a way of expressing bias isn't new. In the 1980s, Fran Rodgers built a multimillion-dollar consulting business helping companies adjust to a changing workforce. At the time, she says, there was often an imperative to have a woman in the hiring pool. But regardless of how many qualified women candidates were in the mix, companies would almost always pick the male candidates. When Fran would ask why the man was chosen over the woman, the answer was often vague and subjective. "In the end, it was likeability," Fran tells me, shrugging.

However pervasive likeability has been throughout history, in this moment it feels particularly in focus. It is emphasized in the workplace, where many companies encourage employees to bring their "whole selves to work" and simultaneously evaluate those employees based on their coworkers' perceptions of them. "There's such pressure to be liked by the people I manage because it's such a big part of how I'm evaluated as a manager," Maggie, a midlevel manager at a tech company, told me. "Does your team like you? Do your peers like you? It's all so data-driven but at the end of the day you're measuring people. Your personal stuff and presentation, and wanting to do extra off-sites is how you're measured, which isn't about the actual results. What if you're a dry, regular person who's hitting your numbers? In the past you'd just be promoted based on that. Now you have to sparkle."

Then this workplace pressure to be shiny is reinforced in a larger culture in which we express ourselves through social curation and are then rewarded with *actual likes* for our glamour, our humor, and our candor. With the rise of social media—platforms whose usership is dominated by women—our likeability can feel quantifiable. How many followers do you have? How many of them liked your post? How many times was your brilliant analysis of Wakanda retweeted? Thousands of followers? Hundreds of likes? Ryan Coogler, the director of *Black Panther*, actually retweeted you? It can feel so validating. Conversely, slim followers? Few likes? Tweets that feel more like screaming into a void than being in a conversation? It can feel as if no one wants you to sit with them at lunch. It's as though the challenges of adolescence have found a way to haunt us into adulthood and threaten not just whom we go with to prom, but how much money we bring home each year.

As Mitch Prinstein writes in his book *Popular*, "Networked society offers the possibility of an interminable adolescence where, as never before, we can shine a light on those who are popular, create ways to emulate and interact with these individuals, and even raise our own level of popularity through new creative platforms that allow any average person a chance to become the most popular, if only briefly." While "an interminable adolescence" sounds like my own personal hell, Prinstein is right: social media has (to some extent) democratized popularity. Far from the days when celebrity was saved for actors, models, and musicians, now a parent who loves to eat paleo and work out can be an influencer. That democratization has also created the sense that if *anybody* can be a public person, then *everyone* who has professional ambition *should* be one.

Working in concert, it can feel as though we're supposed to do our jobs while being Miss Congeniality, all the while understanding that our colleagues, peers, and perfect strangers are judging us not only on how friendly we were during the company off-site, but on how witty we were in our Insta-story rendering of the group trust-falls.

Now, let's be real: you probably will not like everyone you work with and everyone you work with will not like you. That is okay. While some of your coworkers may become your friends, you spend forty or more hours a week with them because you are all paid to do so. People don't always like working for people. It's not necessarily fun to be told what to do. Plus, people are different, and our differences at work, as in life, challenge us. This will sometimes have to do with your difference in age or gender or race, but sometimes it will just be because you are different people with different and seemingly incompatible styles.

I'm not asking everyone to like everyone else. That is an impossibility. I am asking everyone to consider why they are (platonically) attracted to some colleagues and turned off by others, to question how much of that is impacted by bias, and to ask which opportunities they're giving to whom are predicated not on substance but on style.

WHY YOU'RE HERE

Most books on likeability are about becoming more likeable. This is not that book. There are plenty of other books on that, and, besides, I'm sure you are great (or at least there are a bunch of people who think you are great and as we'll discuss later, that's good enough).

When I began writing this book, I wanted to deliver a message that ran counter to all of the existing books on likeability: rather than teach you to care more, I wanted to teach you to care less. I thought that prioritizing likeability was a personal choice, one that was holding women like me back. If we could care less, we would be free to create more, to do more, to be more.

What I came to realize is that encouraging women to "just care less" is an overly simplistic solution to a complicated problem. Rather than liberating women, framing likeability as a question of individual choice shifts the responsibility back to women. Learning to "just care less" becomes yet another "to do" on the seemingly endless list of female self-improvement.

Likeability—and, more specifically, likeability as a woman who aspires to lead—isn't just a self-imposed burden; it is a cultural mandate that has to be reckoned with. Maybe you as an individual can learn not to care about being likeable, but that does not mean that the world will stop demanding it of you, and penalizing you when you are not compliant. While caring less and returning to your authentic self might be great advice as it relates to lovers and friends, it's untenable for a lot of workers. Getting out from under this false choice between likeability and success won't happen just by teaching ourselves to care less.

This book is informed by research, my own experience of caring a lot and learning what that care has cost me, and interviews with other professional women who have lived these questions of likeability, authenticity, and leadership. I interviewed women at every stage of their careers—women who are fresh out of college, women who are navigating the leap from middle management to senior roles, and women who appear on *Forbes*'s list of the Most Powerful Women in the World.

I interviewed women in business, politics, nonprofits, publishing, technology, entertainment, education, law, and medicine. I spoke with women who are navigating long-standing corporate cultures, and women who are opting out to become entrepreneurs, and in doing so, creating their own workplace norms. These women span generations—from the youngest millennials who reminded me that I am a senior millennial who will never understand some basic functions of Snapchat, to baby boomers who have borne witness to how cultural and social change manifests in change at work. I focused largely on ambitious, professional, mostly college-educated women, since upward career mobility is what so frequently sounds the workplace likeability alarm.

Likeability provided a very narrow jumping-off point for much broader conversations about how we as individuals perceive how others perceive us. Even as someone who prides herself on being self-aware and empathetic, I was often surprised by the things other women were contending with. I'm almost five feet eight and, being relatively tall for a woman, I had not realized how often women who are more petite are treated with less seriousness and less respect. As a fair-skinned Latina with educational and economic privilege, a person who can shape-shift between cultures and contexts, I was woefully unaware of some of the less obvious ways in which black women in the workplace struggle to be seen and heard, much less liked and respected.

This book is divided into two parts. In the first, I point out the traps, the cultural shifts and trends that are making those traps additionally challenging in this moment, the larger cultural expectations of women, and the external and internal prices they pay for contending with those expectations. In the second part of this book, I propose new ways of thinking about these old questions, and offer strategies you can use to help yourself, to help others who face these biases, and to nudge institutions toward doing their part. There is no one-size-fits-all answer to the question of how important likeability should or shouldn't be to you as an individual, nor any one path for navigating success on your terms.

I am not an HR professional, a social scientist, or a management consultant. I'm intrigued by these questions because I am living it, grappling with what it all means, and wondering how we're supposed to make choices about our careers when no matter what we choose we're told we're wrong. And of course I'm a journalist, and when a journalist has questions, we research, we interview, we probe. And we write.

This book is about learning to understand the factors that influence likeability—those within our control, those outside of it—and deciding, for ourselves, how much it matters based on what is most true to who we are and what we hope to achieve. I identify the ways that women are forced to choose between being likeable and being a leader, and the workplace scenarios that most often trigger these trade-offs. I explore the things women would gain if they were measured by something other than likeability. I contend that we can stop internalizing the idea that we aren't likeable enough and focus instead on using our collective power to push on the structures holding us back. And I argue that in order to free ourselves from the tyranny of likeability, we have to shift away from talking about *how* women do their work and focus instead on the work itself. To fully empower women to lead, we have to stop asking women to reimagine themselves and, instead, encourage everyone to reimagine leadership.

CHAPTER 2

The Goldilocks Conundrum

Let's start at the beginning. **When you have a résumé that consists of proficient French and a familiarity with Excel, and a job that is mostly printing and** collating, it can be hard to know how to make an impression. Yes, you have to show up on time, do your job, and do it well. Your boss doesn't care that you have a fancy degree and see yourself as a strategist; she sees you as a one-person Kinko's. Those first few years are challenging: you have to show rather than tell your boss that you're capable of more than your job entails, but you never want to seem ungrateful for the opportunities you're being offered. You want to make an impression but you know that meetings aren't open-mic nights.

As times goes on, as deadlines are adhered to, assignments

meet or exceed standards, and dozens of coffees are procured, you can feel yourself gaining some standing in the office. You're no longer the new kid. In meetings, you sit at the main table instead of the chairs by the wall. You offer your insights and feedback. Once you have workplace accomplishments, you tout them.

If you are a woman, as you rise professionally, somewhere between the entry level and the middle, there is often a moment, or a series of moments, when you are made aware that something about the way you comport yourself is a problem. The actual word "problem" is rarely used, but when you cut through all the BS, that's what it is. A problem.

Laura is in her mid-thirties and has worked in politics for all of her professional life. She is beloved by every team she has ever led. Interns cry at their end-of-the-summer going-away parties because she has become their de facto family. She's got a big smile and she's quick to laugh at others' jokes. She always makes sure that her colleagues feel brought in and included in her decision-making process. She minimizes conflict, including negotiating the situation around the office leftovers thief. She is earnest and sincere, and because of that, no one ever worries that she has a secret agenda.

She's also incredibly effective. She is consistently the most competent and highest-producing member of her team. To be honest, she basically runs the place; she just doesn't have the title.

But as much as everyone appreciates Laura, no one really thinks of her as a number one. When her manager leaves, opening up a senior position that she could step into, she is told that while everyone loves her, she lacks . . . something. Results? No, she delivers. The hours? She puts them in. It's just that she's not enough . . . of something.

She doesn't command enough respect. She doesn't take up

enough oxygen. She isn't seen as authoritative. Part of this is about Laura's self-presentation. She speaks as though she is simultaneously apologizing for speaking. Colleagues, even those who root for her—and who doesn't?—admit that she talks a little too fast and her voice is a little too high. She is told to take credit, to speak up more in meetings, to literally take up more physical space.

Part of this perception of Laura is also a legitimate reflection of her priorities. Although she is very ambitious, strives to contribute and lead, and yearns to be recognized for her contributions, she believes the work matters more than anything else. Her ambition remains contained in a vision board in her studio apartment; it need not be a thing she talks about with others. In other words, she'd rather gouge her eyes out than have someone suggest that she's acting like a show pony, but that means she perpetually gives the impression of being a workhorse.

Laura is told that she's not tough enough, but how is toughness being measured? By who speaks the loudest and uses the most expletives? She may not be brash, but that is only one measure of strength. Laura has clawed her way from her working-class midwestern town to the highest levels of government. She worked through her father's sudden death, never missing a beat. By some measures, Laura may be the toughest person you know. But she's not *seen* as strong and commanding.

She doesn't struggle with being likeable; she struggles with being perceived as a leader. This has real implications for Laura: she's passed over for promotions; she watches jobs she wants go to people of equivalent age and experience; and she's offered deputy-level jobs when her résumé proves that she has already performed at the director level. She even receives job offers that would require her to work under someone she has previously managed.

Laura has been taught to work hard, to keep her head down, and to be kind to others. That is who she is and it has gotten her pretty far. But in her mid-thirties, ready to make the jump to the next level, she is suddenly realizing that her likeability is not enough to hurdle over the perception that she "doesn't have it."

She's not alone. I spoke with many women who have been told that, in some way, they weren't enough. They didn't have "executive presence," or there was a perception that they were "not tough enough."

Could the Lauras of the world change in response to the feedback they're offered? Sure. Women who naturally meet the expectation that they be communal and team-focused can learn to be more direct and more assertive. The Lauras know that and they've generally made some stylistic adjustments. They talk slower. They ask more directly. They stop apologizing. In a best-case scenario, that improves their output and their results, empowers them, and makes them better leaders.

What I heard more frequently is that the focus on their style and their subsequent efforts to change only got them so far. Even when they became more assertive, they were still told it wasn't enough. Even worse, the effort to change and the performance of a certain style of leadership often left them turned around and discombobulated.

And then there are women on the opposite end of the spectrum, women like Michelle. An East Coast native, athletic, with a wry sense of humor, Michelle is also in her mid-thirties.

Ever since Michelle was a little girl, she has never been afraid to speak her mind or ask for what she wants. As a kid, it was a hoard of My Little Ponies. They are still in her mom's basement. As a teen, it was a later curfew (no dice). As an adult, working in consulting, she now asks for higher-ticket items: spots on the most important teams, the most challenging and prestigious assignments, promotions, and raises. She is never afraid to ask and ask directly.

In meetings, she always contributes. She leads with her answer and is prepared to explain how she arrived at it. When she disagrees with her colleagues' assessments about project timelines and budgets, she stands her ground. When the people who report to her do an assignment incorrectly she respectfully but pointedly tells them to do it again. She is fair, but she doesn't sugarcoat things. That feels like a waste of time, especially in an industry where speed matters. Michelle makes hard choices: she has managed out and fired low performers, and she has parted ways with clients who weren't a fit. She knows how to take charge.

Michelle is doing all of the things that are supposedly required of a leader: she asserts herself, she offers direct feedback, and she has clarity of vision. She's also wildly ambitious and transparent about that ambition. She has been clear since the day she was hired that she wants to have impact and influence. She wants to learn from those around her and take on challenging assignments so that one day she will be equipped to call the shots. And why shouldn't she be vocal about her ambition? She puts in the work, she cares about her company and her colleagues, and she has all the skills necessary to be in charge.

And yet, when Michelle is at the very top of the middle management chain, with senior management just out of grasp, she is told in her annual assessment that she's a little . . . too much. Her results are great, it's all there on paper, but the way she communicates with others rubs people the wrong way. She gets the sense that her manager would use the word "bitch" if it wouldn't be an HR violation. Instead, her manager dances around the word by using a lot of descriptors that sound like it: Too aggressive. Too direct. Too comfortable with confrontation.

Michelle walks out of the meeting dejected. At beers later with her colleague and friend Tom, they'll compare notes on their evaluations. Tom's went well. In fact, he was lauded for the very things that Michelle was told to minimize—his aggressiveness, his assertiveness. For Tom, all of those things are seen as big assets.

Sound familiar? You are too much—too aggressive, too assertive, so commanding that you ruffle feathers. You are told that you are difficult. Even worse, it is a thing people say about you but not to you. And this smarts more because you look around and see some of your male peers being celebrated for the very thing you're being penalized for.

Can the Michelles learn to change? Yep. They can learn to thread the needle between aggressive and sweet, smiling as they disagree in a meeting, framing their successes in the context of the team, and asking for a raise ever so gently. If they learn to do it convincingly, they might improve their efficacy and their position within the office. But so often, their natural way—to be assertive—is what is necessary to deliver results. If others around them are able to apply those qualities without fear of penalty, how can the Michelles ever compete? Can they round off all of their edges and still maintain their competitive edge?

Every woman is not exactly a Laura or exactly a Michelle, but they represent the two types of leadership assessments that women get most often. They are either, like Laura, told they are not enough or, like Michelle, told they are too much. Plenty of women, myself included, have (confusingly) been given both sets of feedback. They have—in different contexts and by different people—been told they are either too passive or too aggressive, which underlines just how context-driven and circumstance-specific this feedback is.

And listen, I get it: not everyone is destined to be a number one. But if the path to leadership is hemmed in on both sides of the spectrum, then even the women who are destined to be number ones may never be able to squeeze themselves through the narrow opening that remains. If most women are too much or not enough, who then is just right?

In 1982, Ann Hopkins, a management consultant at Price Waterhouse, one of the biggest global accounting firms in the United States, was nominated for partnership. Ann should have been an obvious choice: she had brought the firm more new business than any of the other eighty-seven candidates who were up for partner, all of them men.

But early the following year, the firm informed Ann that she would not be promoted. Instead, partners placed a "hold" on her candidacy. The problem wasn't her work, they told her; the problem was *her.* She was told that she had "consistently irritated senior partners of the firm." In their reviews, they described Ann as "overly aggressive, unduly harsh, difficult to work with, and impatient with staff" and argued that she needed to attend "charm school." Ouch.

Then, when Ann asked a partner how to best reposition herself so that she might be considered for partner again, his recommendation was, "Walk more femininely, talk more femininely, dress more femininely, wear makeup, have your hair styled, and wear jewelry." (Perhaps it should tell us something that *Tootsie*, the film starring Dustin Hoffman as a desperate actor who resorts to dressing in drag to revive his career, came out the year Ann Hopkins received this advice.)

Ann could have opted for the full makeover inside and out. Imagine it: rolling curlers through her hair, wobbling around in unfamiliar kitten heels, and applying just the right shade of lipstick. Sashaying through the halls of the firm (as a woman does!), smiling until her cheek muscles twitched, learning to bite her tongue when others offered ideas that were clearly ineffective or wrong, and making requests rather than giving orders.

Or she could have said "screw you and screw this" and left the firm. But Ann wanted to make partner, so she stayed.

A few months later, the firm informed her that she would not be renominated. Ann left, and sued her employer for discrimination under Title VII of the Civil Rights Act of 1964, which forbids employment discrimination based on a person's sex. And in doing so, she transformed the parameters of workplace sex discrimination.

The legal fight was arduous; it took seven years. "My kids keep asking how many times we have to win this before it's over," Ann told the press near the end of the journey. The case even reached the U.S. Supreme Court, where the Court decided that Price Waterhouse had based its decision not to offer Ann partnership in part on sexual stereotyping. Price Waterhouse could not prove that—beyond the critiques of her manner and her style—it would have otherwise denied Ann partnership. Justice William Brennan, in his opinion wrote, "[I]n the . . . context of sex stereotyping, an employer who acts on the basis of a belief that a woman cannot be aggressive, or that she must not be, has acted on the basis of gender." Brennan also noted the impossible double bind these gendered standards put on women. "An employer who objects to aggressiveness in women but whose positions require this trait places women in an intolerable and impermissible Catch-22," he wrote. "Out of a job if they behave aggressively and out of a job if they don't."

CONTENDING WITH BIAS THAT IS SUBTLE AND UNCONSCIOUS

Three decades later, many of us will read Ann Hopkins's story and recognize the emotional roller coaster of operating in a way that produces the desired results, only to be told that your way of operating is what is holding you back from getting ahead. While the type of overt sexism and discrimination that Hopkins contended with is now legally recognized as discrimination, it hasn't gone away. Instead it's been largely replaced by a much more subtle, "second generation" form of the same. Today's professional woman probably won't be told to go to charm school; she'll be told to tone it down. She won't be called "sweet cheeks"; she'll be regularly interrupted by colleagues. She won't be told to wear heels; she'll be tasked with office errands that have nothing to do with her actual job.

The bias is more subtle, and while that might seem like progress, it is anything but. In many cases, covert discrimination at work is as bad, if not worse, than overt discrimination. If your boss tells you that you aren't being considered for a more senior role because they don't believe that women have what it takes to lead, you won't need to wonder why you didn't get the promotion. You would know you didn't get the job because you are a woman. (You'd also march yourself over to HR, or to the nearest workplace discrimination attorney.) But if your boss tells you you're not ready, or you're not enough, or too much, you are left to wonder whether there is merit to their thinking. Are your boss's concerns legitimate? Or are you being denied a promotion because he is biased against you?

There's another element of Ann Hopkins's story to which most can relate: the way she is described by her friends is completely different from the assessment of the partners who critiqued her. Hopkins's coworkers turned friends called her "kind" and "gracious." With intimacy, they were able to see her in her complexity. The gruff exterior masked a gentler, softer side. But that essence of who she was, the essence of who we each are, is wrapped up in cultural markers that inform what we expect and from whom.

To the world, and certainly to those firm partners, Ann Hopkins was a cisgender, straight, able-bodied white woman who was a professional, a wife and a mother. With each of those markers come cultural expectations and, often, unconscious bias. When any one of us violates those expectations, when we disrupt what other people thought they could expect, supposed order in a disorderly world, people tend to feel some kind of way about it.

Unconscious bias is the qualities an individual attributes to a member of a certain social group. What makes unconscious bias so tricky, as the name might suggest, is that it develops outside of our own conscious awareness. In many cases, it even runs counter to one's own personal values. Read: you can purport to be "super woke" and work to behave without prejudice . . . and still think mothers belong at home.

Analysis by Catalyst, a nonprofit that helps build workplaces that work for women, found that 88 percent "of white people had a pro-white or anti-black implicit bias" and 83 percent "of heterosexuals showed implicit bias in favor of straight people over gays and lesbians." Certainly not all of those people would admit to having that bias! And those biases don't just exist in the abstract; they affect behavior ranging from split decisions to long-term plans like whom you hire or who leads the country.

Finally, in addition to being potentially unconscious and subtle, there is the basic truth, backed up by sociological research, that people favor people who are like them. It's called "in-group" bias. We prefer other members of the groups with which we identify. This presents a major opportunity for those who identify with the same groups of people who are already in power, and it presents a challenge for everyone who does not.

TOO STRONG; TOO WARM; RARELY JUST RIGHT

Researchers Amy Cuddy, Susan Fiske, and Peter Glick have pinpointed two qualities that form the basis of our judgments of others: warmth and strength.

When we evaluate someone's warmth, we're determining their motives. Do they want to help me or harm me? When we evaluate an individual's strength, we're assessing their will to follow through. Does this person have the capacity to bring their idea—whether it's starting a company or punching a hole through a wall—to fruition?

Warmth and strength go hand in hand: warmth tells us about someone's intentions, and strength indicates whether that person is capable of carrying out those plans.

These judgments of an individual, in turn, influence people's emotions and behaviors toward the individual. A person who is warm but is perceived to lack strength is liked by many, but isn't always taken seriously. These are the Lauras of the world. On the other side of the spectrum is a person who is strong, but is perceived as lacking warmth. These are the Michelles. They are regarded as a threat, evoking envy and fear.

Strength and warmth tend to function like a seesaw: as one quality goes up, the other quality goes down. The trick, theoretically, is to balance out somewhere in the middle. But much like an actual seesaw, hitting that midair mark is harder than it sounds.

Leaders require a combination of these two qualities: warmth, so we trust them, and strength, so we believe that they can take action.

With our friends and romantic partners, we tend to prioritize warmth. We're drawn to people who make us feel like they have our best interests at heart. But in a workplace, a premium is more often placed on strength. For this reason, judgments about an individual's strength can impact hiring, evaluations, and negotiations, and influence who gets to do fancy Don Draper—style presentations and who gets tasked with bringing in cupcakes for everyone's birthday.

If we were each being assessed as individuals that would be complex enough. But these judgments are often informed by our membership in a number of social groups. Older people, housewives, and the disabled are all stereotyped as being warm but weak or incompetent. This, in turn, makes people feel pity for those groups and to disrespect them. On the other end of the spectrum, "model minorities," the wealthy, and professional women are stereotyped as strong but cold. In certain contexts, they elicit envy and dislike.

For women, putting aside our many other cultural markers (we'll get to those in a minute), there is an assumption of warmth. If warmth is a major determinant of likeability, then women might even have a natural advantage. But what about at work, where strength reigns supreme? Just dial it up, right? The challenge is that as women express strength, they are perceived as losing warmth. In proving their competence, they become less likeable.

The critique doesn't need to be explicit to have an impact on others' perceptions of what you have and what you lack. Research shows that even when others say entirely positive things about a woman, what they choose to omit creates impressions of what she is and is not. It's called the "innuendo effect."

Let's say you list a former colleague as a reference. When she receives your reference call, she describes you as "So nice. Really easy to collaborate with. Everyone loves her." Those are all positive, lovely things. Yay, you! But if your colleague emphasizes your warmth to the exclusion of your ability to assert yourself, then that potential employer might infer from the omission that you aren't particularly strong. If you were, the thinking goes, someone would have mentioned it. Conversely, if that coworker describes you as "focused, diligent, and hardworking," it can lead to the impression that you aren't particularly warm. If you were, wouldn't the person describing you say that?

And as we all know, those judgments can also be expressed in very explicit terms. A woman who is "too strong"—is pushy, bossy, a handful, and, most commonly, a bitch. These words get used so frequently that it is easy to become numb to them, but these words matter. As Greta, an academic told me, "If you get called a slut your first week of college, you're marked for the next four years. Bitch is the same. Once you've been labeled, it's hard to shake it."

Once people perceive you to be lacking in warmth, it's hard to come back from that. Let's say you're pleasant. You smile. You take your team out for lunch once a quarter. But one time you do something to make people question your warmth. You're short with someone. You deliver critical feedback. Even if you are in the right, and even if you try to reconcile by bringing in donuts the next day, it's hard to reestablish your warmth. Strength, on the other hand, can usually be restored. Messed up a project? Missed a deadline? Came up short on your target numbers? A new client, a new win, or setting a new record can reestablish your competence after a fumble.

Here's the big, underlying challenge: what is expected of women (warmth and communality) is perceived to be the opposite of what is required of a leader (ambition and self-reliance). So when a woman acts the way society expects a woman to act, she is told she is not leaderly enough. When a woman acts the way society expects a leader to act, she is told she is not feminine enough. She cannot win.

Because a woman is expected to be warm and sensitive, and not to be assertive and direct, then when she *is* assertive and direct two things happen. First, she pays a price for being the thing she wasn't supposed to be. She is derided for being too aggressive. In turn, she becomes less likeable. The next part is even trickier. Because she is a thing she wasn't supposed to be, aggressive, others also *assume* that she's not the thing she is supposed to be, warm. If she is assertive and direct, she can't possibly be warm and sensitive as well.

What I want you to understand is that the issue of whether or not other people like you at work, and whether or not other people see you as a leader, often has little to do with the essence of who you are or the leadership potential you possess. Even the most affable woman will run up against likeability challenges if she is also ambitious and willing to do what is necessary to succeed. Even the most capable woman will have her leadership capabilities questioned if her warmth overshadows her strength.

THE TRAP UNDERNEATH THE TRAP

Whether you are a Laura or a Michelle, and you are encouraged to change, resistance comes with its own penalty. If you refuse to comport to either set of expectations—if you don't step into the role of a leader as defined by someone else, if you don't agree to try to become more or less—you run the risk of being punished for being difficult, or dismissed as a lost cause. People will stop talking about your work and instead talk exclusively about you. It will become your own fault that you don't succeed because you refuse to play the game.

Plenty of women know this, and they go along with a lot of BS to avoid being dubbed difficult.

Tracy Chou, a software engineer and advocate for diversity

in tech, found herself working alongside someone who, years prior, she had interviewed and decided not to hire. Her now coworker was still upset about it, so much so that it was affecting their working relationship. Managers suggested that Tracy and her coworker go through a mediation.

"It really felt like I had no choice because if I didn't agree to a mediation then I would be admitting that I was difficult to work with," Tracy tells me. She was trapped.

The mediation included a number of exercises intended to allow both Tracy and her coworker to "let go" of the past events and to begin anew. At one point, the woman leading the mediation threw her arm around Tracy's shoulders and told her, "We women, because we birth children, are physiologically more inclined to hold strong feelings towards other people, including grudges. So, we've just got to let that go!" Tracy managed not to laugh or cry or fall out of her chair (but you can feel free to do it on her behalf!).

"I can't say anything in response to this," Tracy recalls thinking. "If I respond negatively, then it's proof that I'm a difficult person to work with. So I just have to grin and bear this."

Knowing that the field is uneven, how you choose to play the game is up to you. Sometimes marginal edits in style can make us more persuasive, dynamic leaders. Other times that stylistic feedback, taken too far, robs us of the very qualities that make us uniquely situated to lead.

I have been on the receiving end of stylistic feedback more times than I care to count. Some of that feedback, such as cheerfully reframing complaints as positive requests, has made me a better employee (and a better human). But much of it has served as a way of diverting attention from the actual problem at hand. ("Yes, there is no budget for the project we are asking you to complete, but have you thought about the tone with which you're bringing this problem to our attention?")

I have also been guilty of trying to help women I manage by encouraging them in the direction of both being more and being less. I really thought I was arming them with skills that would allow them to be seen as leaders in others' eyes. My intentions were good; my results were not.

In one case, my feedback was a cosmetic fix for a misfit; a skilled person in the wrong role. I wanted her to bring more creativity to her assignments, and to inspire the same in her team. What I *really* needed to say, "We have to reconcile our different visions of success and conflicting beliefs about what is possible within the parameters of our work environment," felt too direct. (My assumption that she couldn't handle that feedback is a form of bias we'll get to in a bit.) Instead of focusing on outcomes, I focused on her style. I coached her to give her team more encouraging feedback. I pushed her to speak up more in high-level meetings. But even when she attempted to do those things, we were ignoring the fundamental problem: our mismatched expectations.

In another instance, I had an entry-level employee who went above and beyond to get the job done, but was frustrated that her responsibilities were disproportionate to her decision-making power. That dissatisfaction bubbled over into tense exchanges and avoidable mistakes. I offered what I thought I could at the time: ways to be less intense in her communication around her frustrations. But that served no one; the frustrations were still there.

When have you been on the receiving end of this bias, and when have you, consciously or unconsciously, directed it at others? And how do these questions become more complicated, in the counsel we give and the counsel we receive, when they are overlaid with other elements of our identity?

CHAPTER 3

Likeability and Authenticity as Luxuries

Whether you're a Laura or a Michelle or anywhere on the sliding scale in between, you have likely received feedback around your work that focuses on style over substance. Even if much of the feedback is well meant and intended to empower women operating in male-dominated environments to best position themselves to succeed, the hyperfocus on *how* women lead is getting us twisted.

Amanda is in her mid-thirties and has worked in finance and tech—industries that are dominated by men. Throughout her career, Amanda's leadership and communication style has been a topic of constant conversation. When she was an associate at a prestigious investment firm, a communications coach suggested that Amanda drop her voice an octave in order to command more respect. Amanda doesn't have a particularly high voice, and yet the thought of her speaking in gravelly tones isn't convincing; it's wince-worthy.

The constant feedback about her style has made Amanda feel as though every decision she makes—from how she dresses in the morning to how she sits in her chair during meetings—is riddled with implications. She's developed a work uniform of dark button-downs and black pants that fit well but not *too* well. She tries to slow her cadence in order to be taken more seriously. She drapes her shoulders over her chair to make herself appear larger and more commanding. It doesn't always work. "I have gotten distracted in meetings trying to do these fucking power poses," she says with a laugh.

By all appearances, the performance is believable. Amanda has ascended to the highest level of her tech company. Plus, she seems genuinely well liked by her peers. She very well could be a unicorn. She is the one who is hitting the mark! She's tough! She's warm! Maybe she's born with it; maybe it's *HBR* case studies.

And yet Amanda admits that she's *exhausted*. It's not the demanding job that is depleting her; she thrives on that pressure. It's not balancing her work life and her home life; she feels her life is messy but exciting. She's tired because she's constantly doing a well-curated performance of leadership that is not entirely authentic to who she is.

"From a professional development and career advancement perspective, this has taken up most of my mind share for the last several years," she says of cultivating her leadership style. "When I implemented all of the feedback, I would then get feedback that I was being inauthentic. It's a double bind that plagues me to this day."

All of the feedback and all of the effort to put the feedback to good use have left Amanda confused. "I'm embarrassed to tell you this, but there have been moments in my career when I've had to take a step back and be like, but who is the authentic me? I don't even remember anymore," Amanda admits. "For as long as I can remember I have been told that I am too X and I need to be more Y. It's all gotten conflated into this desire to be better, and to be liked and to be effective, and to be *seen* as effective, with me contorting myself into all of these different people's expectations of how I should behave."

I ask Amanda if she now knows who her authentic self is.

"Someone who really values making a serious impact on the world by bringing out the best in other people, making the hard decisions and having the tough conversations when need be," Amanda responds. Then her voice shifts. She knows that is a bullshit answer. "I don't even know. I just gave you CEO interview talking points."

Authenticity, we're told, is the key to likeability. But we're also told that we need to perform in a way that makes us likeable. So, which is it? In trying to be more, has Amanda made herself less? What if you have to choose between being you, being likeable, and being perceived as a leader?

This trap—the pursuit of likeability at the expense of authenticity—is to me the biggest and the most all-encompassing pitfall for several reasons.

For starters, the conflict between likeability and authenticity can extend well beyond work to every aspect of our lives.

Maybe you want to be candid with your friend about the fact that she only ever seems to talk about herself, but you know that with that truth comes the risk of alienation. Maybe you lose hours to anxiety wondering if that thing you said about gender reveal parties (while true!) was awkward. Maybe you wear culottes even though they are flattering on *literally no one* because you are embarrassed by the depths of your norm-coreness.

Plus, as one enters the workforce, or new workplaces, and evolves in response to those influences, sometimes a new, *more authentic* self emerges. I spoke with several women who, by working in environments in which they were encouraged to communicate more directly and assertively, actually felt *liberated* to be more direct and assertive. For them, a work environment that was stylistically different from the culture in which they were raised, or the long-standing expectations others had of them, helped them uncover a style that felt more aligned with who they actually are.

In those instances, the growing pains of discovering one's true self manifest in real life, not in work life. Multiple women told me that as they became more assertive communicators at work, a change in themselves that they sometimes liked, people in their personal lives noticed and resisted.

Priyanka, an accountant, works on an audit team with a lot of bold and brash personalities. To thrive, she's learned to be more assertive and confident in the way she communicates. She *likes* the new her. She feels empowered. Her mom, however, isn't so sure. "You always sound so harsh now," Priyanka's mother recently commented to her. "Your tone is always so quick and sharp. You used to be really bubbly." Priyanka assured her that the change was a positive one. "I told her that I'm not bitter and I'm not sad," Priyanka explains. "I'm just getting it done."

The tension between wanting (or, for practical purposes, needing) to be well liked and being one's authentic self at work is the most interesting to me because it is the conflict that becomes most internalized. It can take a serious toll on a woman: her energy, her confidence, her authentic sense of self. With every other supposed choice—warmth versus strength, self-advocacy versus likeability, ambition/success versus likeability—you are really choosing: Do I want to succeed as myself or do I want to succeed as someone else? Can I succeed as myself or is the only way I can succeed as someone else? And am I okay being myself, if that creates an impediment to my success? Or am I okay being someone else?

Plus, it creates a circular pattern. To be a leader we must be authentic, but others either see our authentic selves as not-leaderly, or they see our authentic selves as leaderly but unlikeable. No wonder professional women are tired.

"THAT'S SO WHITE OF YOU"

In the spring of 2018, I participated in an empowerment workshop for adolescent girls. The event was like the quinceañera I never had: there was a DJ, a balloonscape, a catered lunch, a swag bag, and the effervescent energy of teenagers.

In my breakout session, I asked the girls to gather near the front of the room. Half of them eagerly pulled their banquet chairs right to my knees or sprawled themselves on the floor. The rest needed to be persuaded. I opened with a question: "How much do you care what others think of you?" One girl's hand shot up immediately. She energetically talked about the pressure to please people. Others expressed more ambivalence; there were times when others' opinions of them mattered, and times when they felt confident standing in their truth.

Then I asked them to spend time writing about what that

attitude earned them, and what it cost them. Most of the girls joined in, their heads down, pencils furiously scribbling like it was a timed test.

But a handful of girls, mostly clustered around one table, leaned back in their chairs, disinterested. I have interviewed celebrities and presidential hopefuls, but there is no one and nothing more intimidating than a teenage girl. I made my way over to them through the matrix of chairs. "Are you over this?" I asked, a thirty-four-year-old woman searching for the parlance of my youth. No one wanted to make eye contact with me. "Please?" I implored them. Finally one girl, arms crossed, eyes barely meeting mine, spoke up for the group: "Likeability is something that white ladies care about to feel better about themselves."

If this had been captured on video and shared on social media, the caption would have been, "Where's the lie?" For many, a preoccupation with likeability is a luxury they simply cannot afford because they know that they cannot win.

When I told a friend, a black woman, that I cared about being well liked, she sighed and said, "That's so white of you."

What she meant—I think—is this: it's a privilege to even imagine that you have the ability to fit in with the majority culture. That privilege is so deeply ingrained in you that you take it for granted. It is a privilege to *not* feel that your body and your existence in the world are things people reject. It is a privilege to feel that so deeply that you have the time and energy not just to focus on people allowing you to exist, but to like the fact that you do. Forget about success. Just walking down the street, it's hard to worry about people liking you when you know that there are people on that same street who hate the fact of your existence.

My own experience as a straight, white, highly educated, able-bodied Latina had allowed me to believe that likeability was in reach, even within white power structures. If anything, as a cultural shape-shifter, I learned to make others comfortable so that we are both less uncomfortable. Never feeling I belonged anywhere, I have used being well liked as proof that I can fit in anywhere, no matter how true or untrue I know that to be. In my own quest to be likeable, I had not sufficiently considered what it would be like to approach workplace likeability without the presumption that it was even a remote possibility.

To be an ambitious woman who strives to lead creates its own challenges. But in the workplace, those challenges are further complicated by a number of other identities.

AN ANGRY BLACK WOMAN, A FIERY LATINA, AND A DRAGON LADY WALK INTO A BAR . . .

In 2014, *New York Times* television critic Alessandra Stanley ignited a firestorm with a piece about television show runner, creator, producer, and writer Shonda Rhimes. At the time, Rhimes was best known for the television megahits *Scandal* and *Grey's Anatomy*. In the first line of her piece Stanley writes, "When Shonda Rhimes writes her autobiography, it should be called 'How to Get Away with Being an Angry Black Woman.'" It was a problematic play on the title of the new show Rhimes was executive-producing at the time, *How to Get Away with Murder*. Stanley insisted in the aftermath that the point was to praise Rhimes "for pushing back so successfully on a tiresome but insidious stereotype." But most commenters did not see it that way, including Rhimes herself. "How come I am not 'an angry black woman' the many times Meredith (or Addison!) rants?" Rhimes tweeted about two of the white women characters on *Grey's Anatomy*.

That rhetorical question had several possible answers, but

this is the one most relevant to women of color in the work-place: a woman's words can be interpreted very differently depending on her race or ethnicity. Women of color contend with an even more complicated set of expectations than white women.

For black women, assertiveness is dubbed aggression or, even worse, anger.

Consider Serena Williams, one of the greatest athletes of all time. "I feel like people think I'm mean," Williams told *Vogue*. "Really tough and really mean and really street. I believe that the other girls in the locker room will say, 'Serena's really nice.' But Maria Sharapova, who might not talk to any-body, might be perceived by the public as nicer. Why is that? Because I'm black and so I look mean? That's the society we live in. That's life. They say African Americans have to be twice as good, especially women. I'm perfectly OK with having to be twice as good."

But does she have to be twice as nice?

Throughout Williams's career, commentators have dubbed the tennis great overly emotional and, at times, unsportsman-like. She has often been painted as angry. Yes, she's cracked a few rackets over the years. And yes, there have been some on-the-court outbursts. Most notably, at the 2009 U.S. Open semi-finals, Williams responded to what she believed was a bad call by a line judge by yelling, "I swear to God. I'll f-ing take this ball and shove it down your f-ing throat!" Immediately after, she refused to apologize, saying instead, "How many people say things against line judges?" A few days later, she did apologize. She was also fined and put on a two-year probation.

Others mused that she needed to get out of her own way, and expressed confusion as to why she wouldn't rethink her off-court behavior in the name of likeability and corresponding marketability.

There it is, the trap underneath the trap: If she doesn't get to the top of her field, or if she's not compensated the way she could be compensated, then it will be on her for not choosing to abide by a set of standards that were built without her in mind. We tried to tell her to be nice.

In more traditional workplaces, these same biases exist, and they are exacerbated by the reality that a black professional woman is very often the *only* black woman in a room.

Periodically, the managers in Adaora's department gather to share insights and feedback. On one occasion, a fellow manager used racially coded language to describe a member of Adaora's team. Immediately Adaora knew she needed to shut it down.

She asked how the commentary was relevant to the employee's performance. There was no good answer. And rather than address the incendiary language (which Adaora describes as egregious enough to warrant an HR intervention), the focus turned to Adaora. She was told that she was too aggressive in the exchange. Adaora refused to accept the characterization.

"How was I aggressive?" she probed, "Did I shout? Did I scream and call people names?" Her peers conceded that she did not. Rather, it was the act of being the only black person in a powerful room and daring to call out an inappropriate comment that made Adaora the problem.

When it comes to understanding the complexities of being a black woman, scholars debate the virtues of two conflicting models. There is "double jeopardy," the idea of dual discrimination, disadvantage accumulating with each of a person's minority identities. Under this model, scholars argue that a black woman, for example, is worse off than a black man or a white woman, because she faces racial bias *and* gender bias. And there is also research that suggests that when black women demonstrate a dominant leadership style, they are not penalized the way a white woman or a black man might be.

Even if that is true, there are still plenty of penalties for black women. Just because one's leadership style isn't questioned doesn't mean that competence is assumed; minor mistakes at work by black women can be offered as proof that they are not up to the task or suited for leadership. Perhaps worse, a black woman who strives to lead runs the risk of simply being invisible.

For Latinas like myself, the bias is that we're either so meek that we aren't perceived as power players or emotional to the point of being irrational.

During Supreme Court Justice Sonia Sotomayor's confirmation hearing, her temperament became a central part of the case against her. She was called "angry" and "aggressive" and referred to as "a terror" and "a bully." "You stand out like a sore thumb in terms of your temperament," Senator Lindsey Graham told Sotomayor during the hearings. "I do ask tough questions at oral arguments," Sotomayor replied coolly.

Even after Sotomayor made it through the confirmation gauntlet—in large part by offering a disciplined and rote presentation that was more boring than explosive—her actions from the bench continued to be caricatured. Following Sotomayor's dissent in a case addressing affirmative action, her response was described by critics as "overheated" and driven by "emotion."

Calling a woman "emotional" is a great way to call her incompetent without having to use the word.

Asian-American women face a unique bind. Asian-Americans in general are perceived as being more competent but less warm than whites. Recent analysis of Harvard's admissions practices showed that the college consistently rated Asian-American applicants lower than others on positive personality traits, including likeability. Yet that perception of competence doesn't absolve Asian-American women of needing to prove themselves. Asian-American women report that they are asked to demonstrate their competence more than white men.

At the same time, Asian and Asian-American men and women are expected to act submissively. So while their assumed competence makes them sought-after employees, the expectation that they will be submissive limits others' perceptions of them as leaders. One study of Bay Area technology companies found that although Asian and Asian-American women represent much of the tech workforce, they are the least likely to be promoted to the executive level. Great worker bees; not leaders.

And if Asian-Americans act assertively at work, it manifests as a likeability problem, regardless of gender. One study found that given the choice, employees would prefer to work with a nondominant or dominant white colleague, or a nondominant Asian colleague, over an Asian colleague who behaves dominantly. In other words, when Asians act firmly and forcefully—when they act like a leader—they are perceived as being less likeable.

For Asian-American women, this specific bias is most extreme because white Americans typecast Asian-American women as feminine and meek. So those women are under enormous pressure to meet that expectation, and they face incredible pushback when they don't comply.

One consequence of these biases is that women of color often struggle just to have their voices heard.

In 2008, Cecilia Muñoz joined the Obama White House as director of intergovernmental affairs. Cecilia had spent twenty years advocating for immigration reform, she was dubbed a *genius* by the MacArthur Foundation for her work on civil rights, and she was recruited by the president to play a critical role in his administration. Despite those accomplishments, she still had to fight to be heard.

"Just about every day, I felt like I was struggling to have the authoritative voice that I needed to do my job well. Some of that was because some of the people in that building mistook graciousness for lack of strength or lack of authority," Cecilia explains with a sigh, recounting her time at the White House. Indeed, Cecilia's leadership style, expressing warmth as its own form of strength, was in sharp contrast to the tone set in the early days of the Obama administration. The *Washington Post* called the West Wing a "well-documented bastion of testosterone" both for the number of men in leadership and for the nature of their leadership.

The issue wasn't unique to Cecilia. "Women, particularly women who did not have a prior relationship with the president, got drowned out by the testosterone," Valerie Jarrett, senior advisor to President Obama, told me. "He had to be very intentional about signaling to them that part of their job was getting in there, fighting for their opinion, and making their case. The message was, 'Don't shrink because then you're not serving me.'"

Early in the 2016 presidential primaries, many observers, including some of Cecilia's White House peers, dismissed Donald Trump's candidacy. Cecilia, once dubbed "President Obama's conscience on immigration," cautioned her colleagues to take Trump and the potential consequences of his anti-immigrant rhetoric seriously. Every time she made her case, she felt that her argument was overlooked. "The (largely) guys who were the political operatives looked at me like, 'She doesn't know what she's talking about.'"

The one person who did understand what Cecilia was struggling with was Valerie, often the only other minority woman in the room during these exchanges. "I remember her unbelievable frustration," Valerie said. "Cecilia understood that she was not doing her job unless she could get them to hear her."

After a lot of early-morning laps around the National Mall spent refining her argument, and sessions with Valerie, Cecilia got the men in the building to listen. "It took me two weeks to say it in a way that got heard, where I saw the lightbulbs going off over their heads," Cecilia explains. "But for me the only way to do it with integrity is to find an analysis that people will accept." Cecilia put in weeks of work behind the scenes . . . just to be heard.

Dr. Risa Lavizzo-Mourey recalls one telling experience from her time as a clinician and professor at the University of Pennsylvania. She had been asked to consult on a patient's treatment. Later, as the fellow working under Risa reviewed the patient's chart, he noticed that no one had followed through on Risa's recommendations. When he asked another male fellow why the doctor's notes had been ignored, he responded, about Risa, "Oh, you mean the little black girl with the ponytail?" Knowing that these things are said about her, but not to her, Risa is more assertive. "It's the kind of comment that creates a resolve to make sure that when I recommend something, it is going to be the best recommendation possible."

Women of color receive regular reminders that their competence is not assumed, their opinion is not held in equally high regard, and that they will always need to prove themselves again and again.

Class comes into play, too. Williams and Sotomayor each made their way from poor, urban centers, Compton and the Bronx, respectively, to some of the most elite institutions in the world: Wimbledon and the Supreme Court. They are both prime examples of "social hierarchy reversal"; they are members of low-status social groups who have ascended to power.

Women like Serena Williams and Sonia Sotomayor aren't *supposed* to gain access to these elite spaces, and they certainly aren't *supposed* to gain access by doing things their way.

Saying that a woman who has climbed her way to the top of her field with a combination of extraordinary talent, tenacity, and hard work is "angry" strikes me as a lazy way of attempting to remind her that she does not belong, and a petulant expression of resentment that against all odds she has somehow made it without spending the entire time sweating how others perceived her.

LGBTQ BIAS

Despite social gains, discrimination against LGBTQ individuals remains rampant. One in five LGBTQ people report being discriminated against when they apply for jobs, and more report discrimination when it comes to compensation, or being considered for opportunities to advance. The numbers are even worse for LGBTQ people of color. They are twice as likely as white LGBTQ people to say that they've experienced that type of discrimination.

More than half of LGBTQ workers in the United States are not fully out at work. If you're not queer and that doesn't seem like a big deal to you, think about how much of your free time at work is spent fielding questions about your personal life. "What did you do this weekend?" is already one of my least favorite office pleasantries. Imagine having to avoid the question or lie about what you did . . . every Monday. Think about the photos on your desk or the screen saver on your phone. Imagine the energy it takes to carefully omit, to not slip, to constantly hide elements of who you are. Compound that with offhanded comments and jokes ("Bisexuality isn't a real thing" and "How lesbian *are* you?" were two examples offered to me by Meena, a woman in her mid-twenties who works in what she describes as a "diverse, young" office in a creative field) and the standard career advice about leadership seems secondary, by a mile, to the everyday challenge of keeping your shit together.

When Marcy, a supply chain director in her fifties, was younger, and not yet out as a lesbian at work, she kept a picture of her girlfriend's brother on her desk and told coworkers he was her boyfriend. (Luckily for Marcy he was a marine, so deployment was an easy answer to why he never seemed to be around.) She also recalls being invited by female coworkers to go to a male strip club and having to feign interest in the dancers. Think about how much effort went into that performance!

And would you like to know the two reasons LGBTQ workers most often cite for not being out at work? Not wanting to make others feel uncomfortable and the fear of being stereotyped.

So what about lesbian, bisexual, women-identifying femmes, trans women, and queer women who don't just want to be allowed to exist in the workplace, but who want to lead? LGBTQ workers are more likely to be told that their style needs to be more feminine or more masculine.

DISABILITY

The Americans with Disabilities Act (ADA) guarantees legal protections for disabled workers. It guards against discrimination in all aspects of employment, from hiring to training, and it mandates reasonable accommodations. Yet disabled workers face unique questions of when and how to disclose their disability, and in the case of invisible or nonapparent disabilities, a distinct form of covering: *if* to disclose at all. Even once a worker discloses a disability, they often find themselves navigating a workplace where reasonable accommodations are interpreted as "special privileges," and where in advocating for themselves, they challenge others' expectations.

Rebecca Cokley served as the director of priority placement for public engagement during the Obama administration. In that role, she recruited candidates for White House jobs. Cokley, who was born with achondroplasia, the most common form of dwarfism, recalls that when she would meet applicants for the first time, many could not hide their surprise upon realizing that she was a little person. One applicant told her, "I find handicapable people like you so inspiring!" and then attributed Cokley's post to her having likewise inspired the president. Cokley did her best not to roll her eyes, and instead owned the hard work she had put into earning her position. "I manage five hundred constituent groups across civil rights areas," she told them. "I came to this role through the campaign and hard work, just like everybody else." The applicant was shocked.

Disabled women must assert themselves in order to be seen as the competent leaders they are and to get what they need in order to do their jobs. And yet that type of self-advocacy violates the expectation others have of them based on both their gender and their disability.

"People expect you to be a certain way because you are disabled," Vilissa Thompson, a social worker and a disability activist, tells me. "If you are 'aggressive' or very vocal, that's not how people see [disabled people]; as folks that have our own opinions or can handle conflict. Likeability can be a catch-22 because it can lean into those stereotypes of who we are. If we don't fit that stereotype, then that puts our likeability in jeopardy."

Those expectations get even more complicated when you layer on other identities. Thompson, for example, says that racial bias in her work as a disability activist, a space she argues is still dominated by white, male leadership, is more prevalent than disability bias in her social work.

"Many of us experience a lot of sexism, racism, queer phobia, and transphobia in disability spaces," Thompson explains. "For me, being a very vocal black disabled woman, I've had to be more confrontational in some instances, specifically with other disabled white men and white women where they crossed lines and projected their biases, prejudices, and sometimes blatant racism."

MOTHERHOOD

When I was pregnant with my daughter, I worked in an office where everyone was so young and there had been so few coworker pregnancies that I roamed the hallways with cans of ginger ale and sleeves of saltines, sometimes even openly puked into communal garbage cans, and no one suspected a thing. My colleagues probably assumed I was hungover . . . for four months.

One of my greatest reservations about becoming a mother was concern about becoming a mother in the eyes of other people. It felt so deeply othering that I imagined I'd be unrecognizable. "Do you know Alicia?" a new coworker would ask. No longer would the proper response be, "The girl who is always fighting with the vending machine?" It would be replaced instead with, "Oh yeah, she's a mom, right?" I was particularly anxious about the people I'd meet for the first time after having become a mother—people who would never know me as a person in the world without a child. Motherhood is such a powerful identifier that I imagined it would be like the blinding studio lights I was accustomed to—bright enough to blot me out and leave nothing but one dimension of a formerly multidimensional person.

Most of my markers of momness predate my actually birthing a child. I've been falling asleep at 9 p.m., wearing ill-fitting jeans, and neurotically reminding others to look both ways when crossing the street my entire life. But beyond my own anxiety about wanting to seem (and be) independent, portable, and free, there is actual legitimate bias against mothers.

Being a mother exacerbates gender norms. It basically underlines your femaleness, so that everything we've already discussed is on full blast. "If she's warm and kind (and she must be, after all, she's a mom!)," the thinking goes, "then she must not be as competitive or dominant as we'd need the person to be in this leadership position." Then, with those perceptions of "lack of fit" between what the job demands and what a woman brings comes the expectation that she just won't be able to perform the functions of the job. These perceptions and judgments of working moms (especially those in male-dominated fields) mean that we are seen as less competent and, thus, less likely to be given opportunities to advance.

In one study, participants were given details about four individuals, all of whom were said to be applying for a promotion in their existing organization: two parents (one man, one woman) and two nonparents (one man, one woman). Gender and parenthood aside, the applicants were pretty much the same. They were about the same age, they had the same levels of experience, and they held the same degrees. Their supervisors said nice things about all of them.

The mom and the dad applicant took a similar hit: participants expected them to be less committed to their jobs than the two nonparents. Children bring many blessed things, including distractions (my child is literally pulling at my sweatshirt as I type this) and competing priorities (pediatrician visits, bath time, basketball practice). So mothers and fathers are likely to be thought of as less focused and committed to their jobs than people who aren't parents. But when it came to questions of competence, the mom was the only one to take a hit. Another study found that in addition to the competence demerit, participants were less likely to recommend mothers for jobs, and more likely to recommend that they have lower starting salaries.

This is, of course, bullshit. I've never advocated for myself so fiercely as during my twenty-three hours of labor, and I've never been more direct than I have as my daughter's protector. The extreme irony is that, for many women, motherhood doesn't just dial up one's warmth; it reveals the depth of one's strength.

But research has also shown that efforts to combat those stereotypes can have unintended consequences. Let's say you are a mother and you recognize that there is a perception that you are less committed to your job because of your commitments at home. To prove yourself, you hop back on your laptop after the kids have gone down for the night, and you often rely on your partner or support network to be the primary caregiver. Well, beware, there is another penalty looming. In one experiment, researchers created a series of videos that showed an individual being forced to choose between a work crisis and leaving the office to tend to a sick child. When the individual was a mother who chose to rush home, she was seen as likeable but incompetent. When she stayed and managed the work crisis rather than rush home to her child, she was seen as competent but unlikeable. (The dads? No penalty either way.)

BRING YOUR WHOLE SELF TO WORK

Many companies have purportedly embraced the call to allow employees to bring their "whole selves" to work—to show up in a way that is vulnerable, true, and authentic to them. Rather than checking parts of themselves each time they walk through the office doors, workers are encouraged to show up as they are. Yet among the women I spoke with, it seemed the louder and more aggressively this edict was delivered, the more insistent management was about it, the more it conflicted with women's actual experience.

You can be encouraged to talk about your children and still get an eye roll when you have to run out early because the preschool called to say your kid just barfed on the playground. You can cry at your desk because your mom is sick and still have your boss worry that your personal issues are affecting your work product. You can wear braids and still have office mates ask to touch your hair. You can be told to bring your whole self to work only to realize what you probably already knew: that your workplace hasn't done the work necessary to receive you, and so instead you must continue in ways big and small to "cover."

THE COST OF COVERING

Bring your "whole self" to work may be the aspiration, but the United States is far from there: more than half of workers report some form of "covering" at work—downplaying a part of their identity to minimize potential bias against them. Covering, a term first coined by sociologist Erving Goffman, and further cultivated by law professor and legal scholar Kenji Yoshino, can take many forms. Women dying their grays to hide their age, Spanish-speaking Latinos avoiding speaking Spanish in the office, and a gay man not bringing his partner to a work event are all ways of covering. These practices are, of course, more prevalent among those with more marginalized identities. Eighty-three percent of lesbians, gays, and bisexuals, 79 percent of blacks, 67 percent of women of color, and 66 percent of women more broadly admit to covering.

"You feel like you have to be someone else all the time so that you can be part of the 'culture fit,'" Daisy Auger-Dominguez, a workplace culture strategist who has spearheaded talent and diversity, equity, and inclusion initiatives at the Walt Disney Company, Google, and Viacom, tells me. "That feels like you're being smothered from the inside out." Covering requires daily emotional labor in the form of death by a thousand cuts: being conscious of how you sit or hold your wrists or do your hair or talk about your girlfriend, whether to announce that you are stepping away from your desk for afternoon prayers, or thinking twice before microwaving *arroz con pollo* in the communal kitchen. It is boatloads of energy that could be spent on actual work or actual life.

Covering in ways big and small comes at a cost to you, the individual, and in the aggregate, an incredible cost to the organization you work for. "Companies work so hard to recruit these talented employees, but then they don't feel safe enough to speak up," Auger-Dominguez explains. That has a big price. "When employees can't express who they are, they'll only express what people want to hear. At a time when every industry is being disrupted, and we need every idea to transform organizations, that's the *opposite* of what we want."

The personal and professional impact is even worse when workers get the sense that their organizational leaders *expect* them to cover. All it takes is one dose of side-eye to let an employee know that they shouldn't be *too* authentically themselves. And if employees know that they are expected to cover, that impacts how they view the possibility of future opportunities.

LGBTQ employees should feel safe enough to be out and to do all of the mundane things straight people do, like thumbtack pictures of themselves on a cruise with their partner to their cubicle walls and go on tirades about how their mother-in-law keeps pressuring them to give her grandchildren. A working mother should be able to talk about the lice outbreak in her child's class and how she's spent the last three days washing pillowcases without worrying that her coworkers will presume she can't do that *and* finish her end-of-the-year report. Yet for all the talk about bringing our whole selves to work, many of us don't feel our whole selves are fully welcomed. And still others of us feel that that "whole self" as imagined by others is different than the one we imagine ourselves.

"THE CARDI B EFFECT"

I didn't realize how deeply I had fallen down the rabbit hole of motherhood until I was on the dance floor at one of my best friend's weddings and a song came on that I had never heard. The other bridesmaids knew every lyric (and the song is catchy enough that midway through I too knew the chorus) but it was like an alarm bell went off: tune back into the world or you are going to lose touch fast.

I woke up the next day, my feet sore from dancing in heels, with that track in my mind, on repeat. The song was "Bodak Yellow," the artist was Cardi B, and as has happened before in my life, I was several years late to the party.

We live in a moment when it can feel like everything is manufactured. Sometimes I look at my friends and wonder if they're holograms. In that hypertargeted world where even authenticity feels performed, there is Cardi, the part-Dominican stripper turned internet celebrity turned reality TV star turned world-famous rapper from the South Bronx, who constantly stuns with both her music and her very unfiltered Insta videos. Whether she is a contrived genius, an accidental phenom, or the realest of the real, whatever she brings is resonating. As I write this, she has 42.7 million Instagram followers. "Bodak Yellow," her debut single, has gone platinum seven times over. She is the only woman ever to win a Grammy for Best Rap Album as a solo artist. Sidney Madden, an NPR editor, dubbed the velocity of Cardi's ascent the "Cardi B Effect," and described it as "a branding power rooted in specific authenticity."

So, I wonder, can the "Cardi B Effect" apply to a woman who wants to be a tenured professor or a management consultant? Can a regular-degular girl from the Bronx grow up to occupy the C-suite in a corporation? Can a woman, especially a woman of color, ascend to those levels while still being fully authentically herself? Let's put aside for a moment the incredible socioeconomic, educational, and systemic barriers that a woman of color who grows up in poverty needs to overcome to ascend to a position of power. Let's also ignore the reality that (with rare exceptions) most professional jobs require advanced degrees, which require navigating through colleges and universities, and experiencing the initial cultural rinse-and-repeat of becoming an educated, upwardly mobile worker.

Most professionals outside of the creative fields would never get hired if would-be employers checked their social media profiles, an increasingly regular practice, and found Cardi style missives on waxing or footage of them twerking. Most workplaces have standards of what is "appropriate" that would very much confine the physical and verbal flourishes of Cardi. In the movie *Working Girl*, Tess, the secretary turned executive, needs to tamp down her Staten Island accent and tone down the feathered bangs to be seen as a leader. She's still herself, perceptive and street savvy, but to pass, she has to shorten her vowels.

Rita, a media executive, has a former manager who recently wrote a memoir that included references to their shared place of employment. In it, he made only one reference to Rita, but he got her ethnicity wrong, and then portrayed her as angry.

We all know how well anger works for professional women, and how especially difficult it is for women of color to overcome the stereotype that they are angry. Not only did Rita's manager insult her by misidentifying her (there is a difference between Jamaica and the Dominican Republic) and by caricaturing her, he included no positive details. He didn't highlight her work ethic, her savvy, or her ear for a story. He didn't detail the painstaking hours she put into their shared projects. He made her a one-dimensional character intended to advance his own plotline and make himself the star of a story in which he was in reality an extra. For Rita, who has spent her entire career navigating white male spaces as a black woman, the experience was just additional confirmation that as much as she had performed the niceties of corporate media culture, she would always be one exchange away from being reduced to a caricature of a girl from one of the B boroughs.

Maybe that's part of why people are so intrigued by the "Cardi B Effect"—because we want to believe that someone can be rewarded for being so radically themselves. When many of us walk around the world with a culturally mandated filter, there is something unfamiliar about watching someone else just go for it, and then *get it* precisely because they are the things we've been told we cannot be if we want to succeed. It is a nod to this moment of transition and upheaval: we see the promise of expansive inclusion on the horizon, being pushed forward by a wave of cultural and generational shift, and yet for many of us, it all still seems like a distant mirage.

For women, and for anyone with a minority identity, being told to "be ourselves" at work feels a bit like a dangerous dare. Roll the dice and see if your authenticity resonates. If it does, you might reap great rewards. If it does not, your authenticity will be used against you as proof that you were never a fit.

I've often appeared on Sunday morning political talk shows

as the only guest that is under forty, female, and part of a minority group. I am there, in part, to offer a perspective from an underrepresented sample. I was once encouraged by an executive to convey my youth both in tone and in attire. But anyone who tells you to wear a T-shirt on *This Week with George Stephanopoulos* cannot imagine how intimidating it is to bear yet another marker of difference, another reason for the audience and those around the table to discount your analytical contributions. In those moments, a blazer and a sensible blouse become your armor against anyone who thinks you and your perspective are not worthy of a seat at the table.

One morning, I was sitting in the makeup room next to Democratic strategist Donna Brazile, prepping for *This Week*.

"Can you make me look less tired?" she asked the makeup artist playfully.

"Everything okay?" I asked.

"I never sleep before these shows," Donna admitted.

This shocked me. Sure, I didn't sleep, but I was a relative newbie. Donna had lived through more political history and done more of these TV hits than most elected officials. She could do this in her sleep.

"You know the one day I don't stay up all night will be the day they start talking about page three of the Federalist Papers."

We laughed. I felt better. Imagining Donna Brazile studying a James Madison essay made me feel less lame about my compulsive need to prepare for every possible outcome, however improbable. It also turned my stomach upside down: what if Stephanopoulos asks about Alexander Hamilton's case for a one-person chief executive as outlined in Federalist No. 70?!

A few minutes later, as if to put an exclamation point on my exchange with Donna, Newt Gingrich, the Republican former Speaker of the House, another guest on the panel, confidently rolled into the greenroom and asked, "So, what are we talking about today?"

This is part of the conundrum for those of us who want to be ourselves, want to be liked, and also want to be taken seriously. When organizations tell workers to be themselves, they often ignore the reality of how hard it can be for young people, for minorities, for LGBTQ individuals, and for women at large to develop credibility in the workplace. If you sit at the intersection of any combination of those identities, it can be even harder. We know that when we enter a room, there are assumptions made about us, and many of us go to great lengths to undercut those assumptions. We know that we must always be prepared. We cannot afford to slip up. To us, "Be yourself" can sound like a dare, a safe declaration only truly intended for those who are assumed to be competent, qualified, and powerful.

BE THE TYPE OF DIFFERENT I WAS EXPECTING

Sometimes when we are told to "be ourselves" what we are really being told is, "Be a little bit more of what I was expecting." I am often given the impression—and on occasion am told—that I would benefit professionally from being more, to quote Cardi, "spicy mami, hot tamale" and less Latina-ish Liz Lemon. For me, the counsel isn't makeup and heels, it's a jumpsuit and a body roll. I'm not alone in this. Ingrid, a Latina in Silicon Valley, was counseled that she might advance quicker if she wore hoops and red lipstick. Luz, a femme-presenting lesbian, has been told by coworkers that she's "not *gay* gay."

Again, *be a little bit more of what I was expecting*. Fit into the box. Don't complicate the narrative. Bring guacamole to the birthday celebrations. Blare the Indigo Girls at your desk. Be the type of different I was expecting.

When Adaora was an associate at a prestigious law firm, a white female partner pulled her into her office.

"I want to help you make it here," the partner told Adaora. "I can relate to you. I grew up in a rough neighborhood, too, and so I know what you're feeling." Adaora didn't know how to tell her that while she wasn't rich, she didn't grow up struggling. In fact, she attended boarding school.

Regardless of the partner's intention, the message Adaora received was full of assumptions about who she was and how, predicated on those assumptions, she must feel in an elite workplace. "There was this need to fit black people in general into a box," Adaora tells me. "You grew up in the projects, you struggled, you barely learned how to speak English, and now you're here!" Adaora did not identify with this projection, and it gave her an incredible window into the assumptions that are made about her based on her skin color. "That isn't bring your whole self to work," she tells me. "There's a certain self that they want you to bring: the person who was rescued. I wasn't rescued."

And beyond what coworkers and managers want to transpose onto Adaora, there is an equally complicated response to her natural confidence. Adaora doesn't dabble in imposter syndrome. "I have had run-ins with a certain type of white woman who feels really personally threatened by that," Adaora tells me:

> So even if I'm not having an engagement directly against her, there's a sense of, "How dare you present that way." So you're bringing your whole self, which is confident. That confidence is not meant to take anything away from anyone else. It's like, "Hey, we're awesome, let's all be awesome together." But it's experienced as "How dare you think you're all that."

Adaora believes it comes down to this: an expectation on the part of some white women that a black woman, with her double minority status, should feel less confident than a white woman.

As if being different were not challenging enough, we're supposed to be the type of different that meets others' expectations.

Even if that wise teen is right, and likeability is a thing only "white women care about," it is still a part of the way most workers are measured. In many workplaces, it is additionally perplexing because we are navigating a series of mixed messages: bring your whole self, but know that no one is really ready to receive you. Be authentic, but just know that we already have a notion of what that should look like.

Individuals' lack of awareness of their biases, combined with preferences for those who are like us, harbored in the midst of an ongoing shift toward more inclusive workplaces, means that likeability often becomes a cover for unconscious bias. Saying that someone isn't "a fit" or "a match" can be about qualities that have nothing to do with marginalized identities. Not everyone fits everywhere. But lots of times it has *everything* to do with being in the minority. Much of this bias is subtle and unconscious, but it's pervasive. If white, straight, able-bodied women without children find themselves navigating narrow expectations around how they should behave, those paths to leadership are narrower yet for women of color, for queer women, for disabled women, and for moms. And to complicate matters, these women are often navigating them alone.

CHAPTER 4

Damned If You Do

Even in the face of the aforementioned traps that can hold women back, the Goldilocks Conundrum of being too strong or too warm, and the calls for authenticity and likeability that can feel as though they do not apply to all of us, you have likely chosen to pursue success anyway. *Thank goodness.* And yet the pursuit of that success and the realization of it is a trap itself.

Professional women who make the elusive climb to the top—even those who just *look* like they're making it to the top—will run into the Success Penalty.

The Success Penalty: as a woman, the more successful you become, the less others will like you. Just because. Whether you get there by being warm, or strong, being successful becomes a new demerit. Plus, the very actions ordinarily deemed necessary to attain professional success—seeking power, advocating for oneself, even having exceptional grades—will decrease your likeability.

Here's where the calculation gets really complicated: women, like most people, are taught that in order to be successful, they need to be well liked. So if we have established that women can't be both successful and well liked, but they need to be well liked in order to be successful, is the conclusion that a woman can never be successful?

We know that can't be true. Condoleezza Rice, Angela Merkel, and Sheryl Sandberg, am I right?

But there's a reason we all know their names: there are so few of them who have reached the tippity-top of their respective fields. Being a woman who is both successful and well liked is the professional equivalent of landing a triple Axel: possible, but improbable.

So, you, mere mortal, choose: be considered competent and successful, or be well liked. The woman who chooses success thinks, "That is the first line in my obituary." The woman who chooses likeability thinks, "Yes, but how many people will be at your funeral?"

Of all the choices, false and otherwise, that confront a professional woman, this one—the supposed choice between likeability and success—on the surface has an easy answer: choose success. As Fran Rodgers told me, "If you're gonna spend all these hours working, why wouldn't you want to be successful? You want to end up with some asshole boss who used to be your peer but just played the game better?"

Choose success. Choose it every time, because even though it is not guaranteed, it is nearly impossible to attain without striving for, and likeability is impossible to guarantee.

If only it were that simple!

In truth there isn't a onetime existential decision between ambition and likeability, like picking Door #1 or Door #2. Behind the Door of Success is . . . more doors, lots of doors, a series of micro-choices that women have to make every single day to uncertain effect. And it turns out the doorknobs might be electrified.

For example, the path to success for most people requires self-advocacy, and convincing others that they are worthy of investment. So, do I, in the spirit of self-advocacy that is so important to my success, question my boss's feedback, knowing he might like me less if I do? Perhaps I do, if I've chosen to speed down the path of ambition and won't let a likeability bump stand in the way. But what if offending my boss before a performance review actually *threatens* the opportunity for a raise or a promotion? This is where it becomes important to know that there is more than one Success Penalty.

There is a Success Penalty that is incurred when you become successful. But there is another, more challenging Success Penalty: the one that starts taking its toll the moment you start even *trying* to be successful. It's not simply that a woman becomes less likeable when she takes the throne; she seems less likeable merely for eyeing it, and is penalized for doing nearly every single thing that is required to get there.

Consider the case of Heidi and Howard Roizen. While teaching at Columbia Business School, Professor Frank Flynn presented to his students a case study about Heidi Roizen, a successful entrepreneur and venture capitalist. The study detailed Heidi's experience, as well as the professional challenges she faced. One section of the class received the original case, as I just described it. For another section of the class, Flynn altered one detail of the study: he changed Heidi's name to Howard, and altered the pronouns accordingly. He then asked his students to rate Heidi Roizen or Howard Roizen. Students who thought Roizen was a woman judged her harshly. "Although they think she's just as competent and effective as Howard, they don't like her, they wouldn't hire her, and they wouldn't want to work with her," Flynn explains. Among her demerits? Assertiveness, lack of humility, self-promotion, and ambition. In contrast, people liked Howard just fine.

When Sheryl Sandberg brought Heidi, Howard, and the idea of the "success-likeability penalty" to the masses in her 2010 TED Talk, and later in her book *Lean In*, a wave of essays and studies followed questioning how real the penalty was. While I appreciate those who challenge conventional wisdom, there are also some things that you watch happen enough over your thirty-something years of life that you have to wonder if you really need social science to back it up. As my manager Josanne likes to say, "I don't need facts. I have instincts."

I may not be an academic or a practitioner, but as a woman in the world, this feels pretty obvious to me. Has anyone ever suggested to a woman that a great way to make friends is to be more ambitious? Has anyone offered success to women as a pathway to likeability?

It wasn't just Heidi Roizen's success that made people judge her; it was an underlying belief that the things she did to become successful were somehow wrong.

Most of the discourse around likeability and women in the workplace focuses on women at the very top, but likeability plagues us from day one: in order to get a job, people need to like you. Once you get a job, you want to make a good impression. That can mean feeling pressure to go along with things you know are bad ideas, doing others' work and covering for them, or even just rapidly responding to emails for fear of being perceived as lazy. And then, if you don't want to get stuck in your entry-level job forever, you have to make sure that people know your accomplishments without sounding arrogant, and you've got to negotiate to get more responsibility and more money without seeming entitled. You have to receive feedback graciously, and once you're a manager, give it constructively without alienating the people you manage. At every single step, likeability and self-efficacy are in conflict.

GETTING THE JOB

"You are the definition of 'underpromise and overdeliver,'" Lauren, my friend, tells me. I didn't wow her the first time we met. I'm just not that kind of person.

As someone who doesn't make a great first impression, I find job interviews to be the absolute worst. It's a delicate dance that requires Misty Copeland levels of footwork, not the three years of jazz at Union City, New Jersey's Hollywood School of Dance that I possess. Women are told to be enthusiastic without seeming like a tart, show interest without seeming desperate, talk about what they bring to the table without sounding like they're bragging, all the while knowing that their performance in that moment will open or close doors. No pressure.

This is an especially difficult challenge for women who are pursuing leadership roles. When a man walks into an interview, the interviewer presumes he's competent. When a woman walks in, she has to prove it. To demonstrate your competence, you have to show confidence and ambition while taking great care not to allow your competence to overshadow your warmth.

Oh, and be good, but not too good.

When competent women apply for a job, very often the hiring criteria actually shift away from core competencies to judgments about the applicant's social skills. Rather than focus on what she does bring to the table, such as experience or an ability to get the job done, employers focus instead on what they perceive to be her deficit.

In one study led by Natasha Quadlin, the researchers sent out applications from a mix of men and women with different grade point averages. For male applicants, the GPA didn't seem to matter: men with low GPAs received about the same number of callbacks as men with high GPAs. For women, GPAs mattered *a lot*—but not in the way you might expect.

Women applicants benefited from moderate achievement, but not high achievement. Women applicants with midlevel GPAs received more calls than both lower- *and* higher-achieving women. Male applicants with high GPAs were nearly twice as likely as their female peers to get follow-up calls. College majors mattered, too. Among math majors, male applicants with high GPAs were three times as likely to receive follow-up. That's particularly upsetting when you think of the gender gap in STEM fields.

There is a hiring penalty for high-achieving women. But why? Quadlin followed up with a study asking would-be employers to rate résumés for several traits, including likeability and competence.

When evaluating a high-achieving woman, respondents placed a premium on her likeability. Respondents were more than twice as likely to highlight a high-achieving applicant's likeability when she was a woman. Respondents seemed to *love* moderate-achieving women. According to Quadlin: "Their comments suggest that when women have moderate achievement, they are perceived as competent *enough*, but not the *most* competent, which allows them to be perceived as more likeable than women with higher grades." Bet you're glad you skipped all those college parties to make study guides!

You can imagine the assumptions that are made about academically high-achieving women: that their grades are an indication of their ambition, that they must be high-strung and no fun. It's the "innuendo effect" at play: all I know about her is that she's very high-achieving, so I am going to assume that she is less warm and, thus, less likeable. Meanwhile, for all you know, that high-achieving girl was doing keg stands five minutes before she walked into the interview.

Think about the time and energy that goes into properly applying for a job or preparing for a job interview: An impressive academic record. Friends reading over and reformatting your résumé (or CV, if you're fancy). Writing and rewriting your cover letter. Agonizing over what you can wear that makes you look smart and cool, and not like you borrowed your aunt's business suit. You want to prove you have what it takes to get the job, to jump a level, to be seen as a leader. Meanwhile, the very thing that has most likely brought you to this moment—your undeniable ability to do the job—is the same thing that risks tripping up your chance of landing it.

SELF-PROMOTION

Does anyone feel like their boss knows or appreciates the full extent of what they do? I have friends who will document their workday via social media because they know that their managers follow them, and the time stamps are the only way to broadcast that they've worked for twelve straight hours. (We can agree this is unhealthy, and also agree that sometimes it's hard to know if your commitment and contributions fully register with your boss!)

Doing the work is important, but if no one knows that you did the work, then you run the risk of flying under the radar. To get ahead, you must take credit for your accomplishments.

And in a world where few of us are putting in thirty years in one organization, you have to be able to articulate those accomplishments for people who have never worked with you, but may want to.

Taking credit is not instinctive for a lot of women—getting over that is the first hurdle. As former Connecticut governor Jodi Rell told me, women "just want to get the job done. That's what I think women bring to the table. We just want to get the work done. We don't care who gets the credit." While, when true, that collaborative spirit can lead to results and an expedited process, "not taking credit" ultimately limits who gets credit. For women, that means fewer people ascribe the success to you, and in turn fewer people see you as the effective leader that you are. This is compounded by the fact the work *doesn't* always speak for itself; often judgments about vision, leadership, and contribution are based on *perceptions* of whose vision, whose leadership, and whose contributions yielded the final product.

Even once women can confidently self-promote, they face yet another penalty: they are judged for not being appropriately modest. And they pay a real price for that: they are considered less likeable and less hireable.

NEGOTIATING BACKLASH

In 2014, a woman identified as "W" claimed she was offered a tenure-track position as an assistant professor of philosophy at Nazareth College in Rochester, New York. Attempting to negotiate, W sent the university a list of counter-requests, including a higher salary, a semester of maternity leave, a sabbatical, and class staffing parameters. In that email, she did many of the things a woman is encouraged to do when negotiating: she expressed her enthusiasm at the potential of working at the university and couched her requests by writing, "I know that some of these might be easier to grant than others. Let me know what you think."

What the university did next shocked W: it rescinded its original offer. "On the whole these provisions indicate an interest in teaching at a research university and not at a college, like ours, that is both teaching and student centered," the search committee responded. "Thus, the institution has decided to withdraw its offer of employment to you."

The university did not comment on the story, but it's more poetic than any fictionalized version of a negotiation I could write. A woman is offered a job, initiates negotiations, and then that job offer is taken away, cloaked in the explanation that the applicant's asks indicate a lack of "fit" with the institution's priorities.

This story, hosted on the blog *Philosophy Smoker*, a popular site among philosophy student and young professor types, set off a debate. Many commenters were outraged on W's behalf. But others chafed at W's bravado. They called her requests "unreasonable" and argued that she "overplayed her hand."

"W" paid a very real price for her negotiating: she lost a job offer. But she's not the only one to face blowback for initiating negotiations. Other women I spoke with who negotiated their compensation were told—often as soon as after their first counter—that perhaps they did not really want the job, or that maybe it wasn't a good fit. Even when they would ask for something as basic as a salary that matched their current salary, they were made to feel unreasonable.

Negotiating can have big advantages: one study of more than 70,000 employees in corporate America found that women who negotiate and lobby for a promotion are more than twice as likely to get one. Here's something that might surprise you: men report that they are less likely to ask for a raise. Why, pray tell? Because *they are more likely to believe they currently receive fair compensation.*

Allow me to digress for a minute to tell you how much I hate asking for things. Much of my discomfort around asking is wrapped up in the asker-versus-guesser phenomenon.

"Askers" ask for what they want and need. They will ask you to pick them up at the airport, babysit their kids, or borrow your nicest piece of jewelry. They'll ask regardless of whether you're their lifelong bestie or a coworker whom you've interacted with once. Part of the reason askers are so comfortable asking is that they are comfortable getting a no. If they want to sleep on your couch, they will say, "Hi, I am coming into town on Thursday night. Can I sleep on your couch?" To an asker, the worst thing that can happen is that you'll decline their request.

I am not an asker. I am on the other side of that continuum, a "guesser." I hate to ask for anything. Whereas askers jump in without testing the waters, we guessers wait to ask until we're pretty sure the answer will be yes. In our perfect world, we'd be offered what we want without having to ask for it. So for me, a guesser, the same conversation (let's be honest, text exchange) about sleeping on someone's couch goes more like this:

Me: Hey
Friend: Hey.
Me: The weather, right?
Friend: You're being weird.
Me: So, I'm, yeah, I'm going to be in town Thursday night.
Friend: Oh cool. Do you want to do something?
Me: Yes, definitely. I'm still figuring out where to stay. . . .
[Inside voice me: Please offer your couch, please offer your couch.]

Friend: Well you're welcome to stay with me.

Me: *[Inside: I've already put her out. She's being so polite. If she really meant it there would have been an exclamation point at the end of that text.]* Really? That's not an imposition? Are you sure?

Friend: It's fine.

Me: *[Shit. Two texts with no exclamation points!]* You can totally tell me no.

Friend: But I just told you yes.

Me: *[DO YOU NOT USE EXCLAMATION POINTS?!]* Maybe I should just stay at a hotel *[Maybe you should just stay at a hotel. Also: consider therapy.]*

You see? Neurotic. Painful.

Part of the reason I and other guessers hate asking is that we don't feel that the individual on the other end of the ask really has the option of saying no. That is, in part, because when people ask us, the guessers, for things, we feel obligated to say yes. I have said yes to so many things I did not want to do: hosting house guests, helping people move in ninety-degree heat, even cat-sitting despite a deathly allergy, because all of those painful things seemed less painful than saying no.

All to say: I don't like asking for things for myself. But I do like money, so negotiating already poses an internal conflict.

I know that I'm *supposed* to ask. I *know* the conventional wisdom on this: It never hurts to ask! The squeaky wheel gets the grease! It's as though every upwardly mobile woman is one ask away from doing the backstroke in her Scrooge McDuck–inspired Gold Coin Pool. But shifting the negotiation gap back on women is overly simplistic.

Women often pay a stiff social penalty for asking for what they want or need. Women who negotiate "are more likely than men who negotiate—and women who don't—to receive feedback that they are 'intimidating,' 'too aggressive,' or 'bossy.'" Advocating for oneself, specifically for personal resources like a raise or a bonus, is a dominant act, and for women that conflicts with the notion that they ought to be "nice." And, because women have long been considered to have less status than men, the mere act of saying, "Hey, I think I deserve what he has," can make a woman seem "inappropriately demanding." For both violations—acting dominant and laying claim to equal privilege—women seem less likeable. (In contrast, when men ask for more they pay no price. Men typically earn more than women, so it doesn't surprise employers when they ask to be paid more.)

In experiments around compensation negotiations, a group of researchers found that evaluators penalized women candidates more than men for initiating compensation negotiations; they were less likely to hire those women, and less likely to want to work with them. A simulated salary negotiation study found that participants negotiating with an assertive woman were less likely to want to interact with her—in the office and outside of the office—than with men who asked in the exact same way.

Just knowing that there is a high likelihood of backlash, of being less likeable, women modulate their asks. In one study, men and women negotiated a starting salary with the understanding that they had another job offer of $40,000. At the outset of the negotiations, men and women showed no significant difference in what they hoped to make, but women anticipated blowback if they negotiated too hard. They assumed the hiring manager would judge them if they asked for more than $43,250. Men assumed they could negotiate up to $50,813 without pissing off the hiring manager. When the hiring manager then actually lowballed all the participants, women were quick to concede. They countered, asking for only $42,000. Men asked for more than $48,000.

Those women *knew* what they were doing. They didn't ask for less because they thought they deserved less. They didn't ask for less because they thought their ask was competitive. They reported *knowing* that they were making big concessions, and they made those concessions because they were worried about the backlash they'd face. They knew they had to choose between getting what they wanted and being well liked, and instead they tried to split the difference. That's in the cases where women actually take on the negotiation. Simply anticipating that there will be backlash, women will often avoid negotiating altogether.

Following the Sony Pictures leak, wherein hackers released confidential data, including emails that revealed that Jennifer Lawrence's *American Hustle* costars made more money than she did, Lawrence wrote a piece about how these perceptions and penalties had altered her approach to negotiations. "I got mad at myself. I failed as a negotiator because I gave up early. I didn't want to keep fighting over millions of dollars that, frankly, due to two franchises, I don't need," Lawrence wrote. "But if I'm honest with myself, I would be lying if I didn't say there was an element of wanting to be liked that influenced my decision to close the deal without a real fight. I didn't want to seem 'difficult' or 'spoiled.'"

And because the person on the other side of the negotiation knows all of this, they can use it to their advantage. When Kaitlin Menza got the call saying that she had landed a job at a women's magazine she long admired, she was over the moon. She was also ready to negotiate. As she jokingly told me, "I work in women's magazines, so I've read all the articles." But when she countered on salary, the recruiter balked. She said she'd have to loop back around with the hiring manager to ask her about the increase. "Are you sure you want me to?" she asked Kaitlin. "You'll be starting off the role leaving a bad taste in their mouth. Don't you want them to like you?" Kaitlin later recounted in a piece for *Marie Claire*.

This recruiter knew that she had a powerful weapon in her back pocket: she played Kaitlin's desire for more compensation against her desire to be well liked, and her fear that she would be penalized for asking. Kaitlin admits that she fell right into the trap. She immediately withdrew her counteroffer, begged the recruiter not to bring it up with her future manager, and accepted the original number. Good-bye, 5 percent increase! Hello, subtle sexism.

Years later, Kaitlin told that same hiring manager about the exchange, and that manager was horrified. "I did not know she wanted to ask for more, I would not have been mad or held it against her, and I am upset that anyone would use my influence to make a young journalist feel small and unworthy," the manager told me. The threat of jeopardizing Kaitlin's likeability wasn't even based on a likely outcome; it was simply playing on fear.

So, let's say you do negotiate, and you do get the raise or the bonus or the extra four weeks of vacation time. By one measure, you've won: you got what you asked for. But you might have unfairly lost something more amorphous in the process. What if the negotiation itself left such a bad taste in everyone's mouth that you can't overcome the perception that you are pushy or entitled? How real is that? How lasting is it? Do you then need to work to earn back your likeability? Think about the long-term effects that those outcomes—being less likely to be hired, less likely to have others want to work with you, and less likely to have others want to spend time with you—can have on a woman's career.

And so a woman must assess whether the potential benefits of negotiating (twice the likelihood of a higher salary, a
better title and better terms) is worth the risk of the potential
consequences (a rescinded offer or alienating managers or colleagues who might be critical to her success in the future).

W, the woman whose offer from Nazareth College was with-
drawn after she attempted to negotiate, was just doing what
professionals are counseled to do; she asked. "This is how I
thought negotiating worked, how I learned to do it, and, for
that matter, how I think it should work," W wrote in a follow-up
blog post. "You ask about a number of perks and maybe get
some of them. I just thought there was no harm in asking."
Among the unfair aspects of W's case was the lack of transparency around how and why the decision was made. Why didn't
anyone spell it out, allowing her to weigh her options?

Some of this is situational. A woman who is negotiating
for a personal raise is less likely to face a penalty when she is
higher up within an organization. And when women negotiate on behalf of a group, there is no penalty. Acting on behalf
of others makes a woman seem, well, nice. But what that tells
us is that a woman is not allowed to act in the service of herself.

FEEDBACK

Feedback and reviews are, by nature, subjective, but performance reviews of women employees tend to over-index on subjective feedback. Behavioral economist Paola Cecchi-Dimeglio's
analysis of these reviews found that they are often riddled
with the gender biases we've discussed, as well as confirmation
bias ("I knew she'd have a hard time completing the project on
deadline"). Women are more likely to receive critical subjective
feedback—meaning that for women, reviews and evaluations

are often negative expressions of their manager's opinions of them, rather than positive expressions or useful evaluations of their skills and contributions.

These biases are most noticeable, and most problematic, when viewed in contrast to evaluations of male peers. If Jill is indecisive, but Mark is thoughtful—would you rather work with Jill or Mark? If Nadia is melodramatic but Dante is passionate, whom would you promote?

Women are also less likely to receive constructively critical objective feedback—the type of insights on their work that is actionable and based on substance rather than style. The feedback women receive is often vague and not tied to outcomes. Even when they are praised, they don't receive pointed developmental feedback about what is necessary to make the next leap in their careers. So a woman may walk out of a performance review feeling great, but with no clear sense of what she's doing right or how she can use her existing skills to catapult herself to the next level.

I have received only one performance review in my entire career, and since I just wrote a few pages on self-promotion, let me tell you, it was G-L-O-W-I-N-G. As someone who works hard, wants to be well liked, and worries I'm not, I damn near floated out of the room following that review. But now that I look back on that experience, I realize no one told me how I could build upon what I'd already done or how I could improve. And because I just wanted the validation of being in everyone's good graces, I didn't think to ask.

While we may *need* constructive critical feedback, there is often an assumption that women can't really handle it. "It's awkward to give critical feedback to people in general," Lily Jampol, a behavioral scientist and diversity and inclusion strategist, explains. To mitigate the awkwardness, sometimes people will "upwardly distort" the feedback to make it sound less critical and to make delivering it less painful.

Jampol suggests that it's also possible that those tasked with giving feedback walk into those sessions with different goals, depending on the gender of the person they are reviewing. In Jampol's analysis, those goals are informed less by the assumption that women are more sensitive than men, and more by this idea that women don't have agency and require more hand-holding.

"While people want to be candid to both men and women, they find that people prioritize kindness goals more for women than for men," Jampol tells me. This same dynamic plays out with racial and ethnic minorities. That may sound like a good thing (I, too, like when people are nice to me) but if no one tells you what you're substantively doing wrong, you're bound to continue doing it over and over again.

Finally, when women do get feedback, it tends to over-index on their communication style. Alexandra Wilkis Wilson, senior vice president of consumer strategy and innovation at Allergan, and cofounder of Gilt, GlamSquad, and Fitz, recalls being told early in her career that she used her hands too much when she spoke, and that if she insisted on using her hands, she ought to use them in a "masculine" way, like counting down her points. Ursula Burns, the former CEO of Xerox, and the first black female CEO of a Fortune 500 company, was told that her style of speaking was too fast and too casual. Tracy Chou (the software engineer and advocate for diversity in tech who you'll recall was forced to do that silly mediation) was told by a manager that she should talk more about technical subjects in social settings so that her peers would take her more seriously.

Not only is that feedback often biased and largely unhelpful, it takes up the time and the space for discussing recommendations of what women can do to render measurable outcomes.

PLEASE DON'T HELP

You know those helper tasks that pop up in every office? The coworker who needs help with the coffee machine or filling out a vacation request? Agreeing to help with those tasks is seen as less optional for women than for men. In fact, some studies suggest that when a man is willing to pitch in on those "altruistic" tasks, it creates positive associations among his coworkers. You took out the trash? Gold star for you, Seth! Agreeing to those helper tasks doesn't give a woman the same boost, because people *expect* that she'll be willing to do those things. And, if she doesn't oblige, she actually gets a demerit. You didn't take out the trash, Jenna? You must be a monster.

And even though women are expected to be helpful, they can't be *too* helpful. Studies show that women are perceived to be less task-oriented than their male peers. That's not because they can't focus enough to stay on task; it's because there is an expectation that they'll take a break on a "selfish" task to work on an "unselfish" task—helping Gail reload the water-cooler, or holding Andre's clammy hand while he talks about how the girlfriend he's broken up with three times in the last two months is at it again. If you ask me, this type of work isn't really even that off-task. It's necessary. Have you ever worked in a bougie professional office without filtered water? People would rather just dehydrate themselves than drink from the tap. Do you know how distracting it is for the team when Andre goes through a breakup and forces the entire pod to listen to "Unbreak My Heart" on a loop? The company loses *hours* of productivity. Sometimes days. If a woman can take a quick break from budget reports to tend to Andre's broken heart and fragile ego, shouldn't we all applaud her for her service? Instead, her sensitivity to interpersonal drama is seen as a weakness rather than the public service it really is.

"THIS IS MY JOB. I'M NOT HERE TO MAKE FRIENDS."

There's all the asking and self-promoting stuff that business books talk about. But can we just talk for a minute about the complexity of friendship in the workplace? Like, yes, you likely spend more time with your coworkers than your family, so it's natural that friendships develop. On the flip, you get paid to spend that time together; it's because that time is supposed to be spent in the service of something else.

So what's the correct standard for what is socially mandatory at work? On one hand, I go to work primarily to get my work done. On the other, the only adult friends I have made are through work. But that chitchatty in-between stuff? Hearing about someone's obsession with Minecraft or the politics of their condo board? I really gotta be in the mood. But I know that to be well liked, I need to go with it. And I know that my not-always-tactful honesty ("Dump him") is an acquired taste that requires more intimacy than you necessarily get by spending your lunch breaks with someone.

Melissa, who works in fashion, was once told by a boss, "This office is a sorority and you're a bad pledge." At another job, a boss criticized Melissa for not sharing enough of her personal life with her, and encouraged Melissa to come to her for dating advice. Doesn't that seem. . . . a little much?

My friend Marisol, a television producer, loathes office small talk. "I don't want anyone to ask me what I did over the weekend and I don't want to know what they did over the weekend," she says unapologetically. And yet I have watched as her office mates do what office mates do—recounting everything from day cruises to the *Vanderpump Rules Reunion*. I know her well and so I can see the amount of energy and self-control it takes for her to smile and pretend to nod along enthusiastically.

Marisol believes that her work speaks for itself. She's good. She's fast. She's reliable. Her work, she argues, makes people like her. Unfortunately for Marisol and those like her, research shows that social capital (which you gain from all of that chit-chat, and bowling alley outings and company picnics) is often more necessary to a manager's advancement than hard skills and execution of tasks.

Opting out comes at a price. This is an especially big challenge for parents and caretakers who might not have the time to engage in office banter or dedicate to after-hours office extracurriculars. When you've gotta leave work at 5 p.m. on the dot to make it to pickup, the workday feels as if it is marked by a starting pistol, and any interaction that is not efficient and productive can feel like a hurdle to executing everything on your to-do list before the imaginary end of the day buzzer rings. Sometimes you might even find yourself drifting into *enjoying* an office exchange about March Madness brackets, only to be interrupted mid-thought by visions of your disappointed kid sitting on the curb waiting for you, again. It's also especially difficult to participate in informal networking when you are a minority in your office. 'Cause you know, the *queso* stands alone.

AMBITION

On some level, the American public seems keenly aware of these biases. In 2015, asked by Pew Research to explain what's "holding women back from top jobs," respondents identified biases such as women being "held to higher standards" and resistance to hiring and electing women as bigger barriers than, say, women not being good managers. The research also found that the public regarded men and women leaders in much the same way—with little distinction on intelligence or innovative ability. If anything, the findings showed that women have strategic advantages. In the eyes of the public, women are more likely to be honest, compassionate, and organized.

When you ask which qualities are "absolutely essential" to leadership, men and women put honesty, intelligence, and decisiveness all at the top of their lists. But go a little further down those lists and there are differences. Women are much more likely than men to include "compassion" among those qualities. They're also more likely to place a premium on innovation. And women, especially younger women, are more likely to say that ambition is important.

Ambition—what a double-edged sword! Look at what all the research tells us about ambitious and successful women: they are punished by being viewed as less likeable. Look at what history teaches us: to be a woman who is determined to succeed is to be judged, ostracized, scorned. It is often used to denote that a woman is ruthless, cold, or unstable.

Yet ambition is a form of resilience. It is the motor that powers you through rejection, long nights, and pitch meetings where investors or studio executives or your higher-ups turn you down. A 2014 study by the Center for Talent Innovation found that black women tend to be more ambitious than their white female peers. This doesn't surprise me at all. If the path to leadership narrows for women generally, and narrows even more extremely for black women, then of course a black woman needs an extra strong motor to push herself through.

When you have been historically discounted, if you run the risk of being invisible, of course you have to declare louder and bolder, "I want this and I deserve this." Black women do not have the luxury of being ambivalent or modest about their ambition.

Black women on the path to a leadership position are more likely to view a leadership role as enabling them to "flourish" and "be empowered and empower others." They are also more likely to identify "the ability to shape the direction of their field or profession" and "the ability to exert influence on other powerful people" as critical elements of being in power. Of course, if they have been at the mercy of organizational leaders who do not share their life experience, they want to clear the way for others. (The irony is not lost on me that while women are judged for the supposedly ruthless, selfish fact of ambition, they identify *helping others* as a prime motivator for seeking power. Sounds wildly selfish to me!)

You know how in Super Mario Brothers, Mario, with the help of a Starman, will become temporarily invincible? You know how it supercharges him through every hurdle along the way? Allowing him to jump higher, to blast through noxious critters unscathed? That to me is the potential power of ambition. No wonder it evokes such disdain.

Without ambition, no woman would ever be propelled to take on the challenges of the firsts and the greats. Without a woman's ambition, there is no Oprah or Ava DuVernay, no Mellody Hobson or Geisha Williams. Even the most altruistic civic and philanthropic leaders have to have ambitions for their cause if not ambition for themselves. It doesn't surprise me that women believe that ambition is critical to being a leader—because ambition is the thing that keeps you saying yes when everyone keeps telling you no.

All of these professional necessities—getting hired, self-promotion, negotiating, receiving feedback, developing social capital, and cultivating ambition—are critical for success, and yet they are all fraught with their own complexities. But let's say you survive the gauntlet; you still have to get through the biggest obstacle: the power grab.

CHAPTER 5

The Power Grab

The likeability of a woman leader is often a thing that is spoken about in hushed whispers. Unless, of course, you are a woman seeking public office. Free, nay, *encouraged*, to give their opinion on women leaders, the media and the public often find they can talk about nothing *except* a woman's likeability.

Sure, male candidates grapple with likeability. Donald Trump had some of the highest unfavorable ratings of any presidential candidate ever. He was called "super-unlikable" and described as having not just a likeability problem, but a "likeability epidemic." Fellow 2016 presidential hopeful U.S. senator Ted Cruz was so unliked that he inspired headlines such as "Why Do So Many People Hate Ted Cruz?" In fact, being disliked so publicly by so many people became a part of Cruz's brand; he used the distinction to positively position himself as a Washington outsider. Mitt Romney, as the 2012 Republican presidential nominee, was called a "malfunctioning robot" and a "disagreeable human being." John Kerry was deemed "aloof" and "emotionless" and widely mocked for his windsurfing, which made him seem extra uncool. Al Gore was described as a "know-it-all," "wooden," and "stiff." Basically, if you know anyone who needs to be knocked down a notch you should encourage them to run for president!

But while male candidates may struggle with likeability, research shows that voters will support a male candidate even if they don't like him, as long as they believe he is qualified for the job. Women candidates face a different test: in order to win, they need to be both liked *and* perceived as competent. And while voters assume men are competent, women have to prove that they are.

When Christine Todd Whitman ran for governor of New Jersey, skeptics suggested that her husband must have been the architect of her tax plan. Earlier in her career, Nancy Pelosi, now the Speaker of the House of Representatives, launched an unsuccessful bid to chair the Democratic National Committee. Her opponents called the Democratic politician an "airhead."

So how does a woman candidate prove that she is competent while maintaining her likeability? According to research from the Barbara Lee Family Foundation, confidence is key. It's a marker of competence and likeability. And time is of the essence. Voters assess a woman's confidence in less than thirty seconds, less time than it takes to reheat a cup of coffee.

When talking about accomplishments, voters like when a woman explains why an issue is of personal importance ("I have kids in our public schools," "I still haven't paid off my student loans," "I have literally fallen into the pothole at the end of this block") or how constituents are impacted by her accomplishments. Voters prefer when a woman both shares credit with her team and takes some credit herself. And on top of all that, voters like when a woman has a sense of humor and "doesn't take herself too seriously."

I asked Celinda Lake, the pollster who spearheaded this important research, if it's really possible to hit all of these marks. "It's definitely possible," she told me. "Whether it ends up making women candidates feel distorted and twisted is another question."

And this is the stuff a woman candidate can supposedly control!

Out of her control? For starters, appearance and race, both characteristics that voters pay close attention to. The more attractive a woman was, the more likeable voters said she was, and, predictably, voters found younger women more attractive. Trump channeled that bias against women when he mocked the physical appearance of candidates Carly Fiorina and Hillary Clinton.

Studies have found that when the press talks about a woman candidate's looks, she becomes less likeable. It doesn't matter whether the coverage is positive, negative, or neutral, whether it's the *Washington Post* describing then governor Nikki Haley dressing as a "Real Housewife: fit, attractive and encased in suits that stop just below the elbow and just above the knee," or Fox News calling then Democratic Party chair Debbie Wasserman Schultz a "frizzilla." It hurts her credibility and her favorability. In one experimental survey, discussion of a woman candidate's appearance lost her points on "being tough, being likeable, confident, effective and qualified."

But when the media talks about a male candidate's looks (which, let's be honest, we're less likely to do because you can use the lines "he was wearing a sensible navy Jos. A. Bank suit" or "he combed his salt-and-pepper hair from left to right" only so many times), men pay no price.

Then, as if assessing a woman's looks weren't problematic enough, there is the dreaded discussion of a woman's voice. Prime Minister Margaret Thatcher was called "shrill and hectoring." Clinton's voice was described as "screechy" and her laugh was often described as a "cackle." According to the research, "Voters are sensitive to women officeholders sounding 'shrill,' 'loud,' and 'boring.'" That's right, women need to talk about tax reform in their EXCITING (yet soft) voice.

There have been some shifts in conventional wisdom about how women project an image of leadership. For the longest time, there was a boring but reliable formula. Imagine a lady in a red power suit with enough shoulder padding to make her look like a linebacker and enough hairspray to likewise sustain impact. She is seated behind a big wooden desk, smiling tensely with her hands folded. Think Julia Louis-Dreyfus in *Veep*. Geena Davis in *Commander in Chief*. Téa Leoni in *Madame Secretary*. (I realize these are all fictional characters. Fiction is the only place where I've seen a woman executive lead my country.) Newer research has found that voters actually prefer images of women leaders in a more casual environment, such as being in conversation with constituents or stock models who perfectly mirror the demographic composition of the district.

So, to recap: be confident, warm, and strong. Tell voters why issues are of personal importance, but also why those issues are relevant to them and their lives. Take credit, but also share the credit. Make sure people take you seriously, but don't take yourself too seriously.

Honestly, the last time I was this confused about what to do was when I had to do the Wobble at a wedding.

As if finding what political scientist Georgia Duerst-Lahti

has called "the perfect blend of pantsuits and pearls" isn't challenging enough, there is an added dimension to this delicate performance: voters' desire for authenticity. "For male candidates, being authentically male means meeting masculine expectations that are most associated with candidates and officeholders," Kelly Dittmar, an assistant professor of political science at Rutgers University–Camden and a scholar at the Center for American Women and Politics, writes. "For women running, authenticity is less straightforward; it is assumed that women, as political outsiders, have to 'act' the part of candidate and officeholder in order to meet both the masculine credentials for the job and the feminine credentials of being a 'real' woman." For women, walking the line between strength and warmth is, by definition, a carefully calculated performance. How can any person exist in such a narrow space and still, somehow, be asked to be themselves?

In 1990, at just twenty-five years old, Jane Swift became the youngest woman ever elected to the Massachusetts State Senate. Eight years later, pregnant with her first child, she campaigned to become the state's lieutenant governor. As if ripped from the pages of *Lean In* fanfiction, she gave birth a few weeks before winning her election.

When Governor Paul Cellucci stepped down in 2001 to become ambassador to Canada, Swift, again pregnant (this time with twins), became acting governor. She gave birth to her daughters one month into her term in office, making her the first sitting governor in history to give birth in office.

Swift's critics asked who would raise her child while she was busy working. Would she really be able to focus on governing while mothering? The questions rang in Swift's ears.

"I had this false choice every day where I could either be labeled a terrible mother or a terrible lieutenant governor," Swift tells me.

What's more, the critiques evolved into an official investigation: questions swirled about Swift's use of staff to babysit her daughter, and her use of a state helicopter to travel home one Thanksgiving. Both issues seemed to answer the question "How is she balancing it all?" with a nefarious answer: she's abusing the power of her office to make it all work. If Swift didn't understand the emotion those issues evoked at the time, she understands it now. "It is really so hard for so many families to feel like they can successfully combine work and family, that feeling that I was getting any kind of privileges that they were not getting in their private lives just resulted in this deep-seated anger," Swift tells me. "I get that."

In addressing those charges publicly, Swift also confronted the conflict between competence, likeability, and authenticity. "I didn't ever cry in public, but I cried a lot in private," she tells me. "There were many a day where a couple trusted staff members and I would run through press conferences of deeply personal issues. I would practice the answers that I had to give and go over them over and over and over until I could have them so well memorized that I could say them without crying." Swift knew that crying carried a cost. "It really felt like the stereotype of a woman crying would've been devastating for me as a woman in a position of power." But not crying also had a price. "I did appear fairly robotic and without much empathy," Swift admits. "But that was the best I could do. I couldn't engender any emotion and prevent myself from being a total puddle when people were accusing me and my husband of being liars and cheaters and criminals and bad parents."

An ethics ruling found that the unpaid babysitting was a

violation, one for which Swift paid a $1,250 fine. The panel cleared her of wrongdoing on the helicopter issue.

Swift faced the bias all working mothers are up against. Warm at work where competence is king. Cold at home where warmth is queen. And then she faced the more specific bias against mothers in politics, the idea that either the job or the family will suffer. When Sarah Palin ran for vice president critics wondered whether she could manage the needs of her five children, including an infant with special needs, and the demands of a campaign. Professor Susan Carroll sums it up this way: "For men, voters view families as a support system. For women, they are seen as an additional responsibility."

Not only are men asked about their families less, but when men candidates are critiqued about their ability to manage it all, they bounce back quickly. Women candidates, when questioned about their family, are less likely to regain whatever ground they lose.

When I connect with Swift, it's been fifteen years since she's left office, but I get the sense that she is still trying to figure out what the lesson in her own experience is for other women. "I'd rather be liked and well respected by the people who actually knew me than by those who are judging me without ever knowing me," she says.

She might also, in the most professionally aspirational version of the Jane Swift story, have been a presidential contender. Think about it: she was a young, moderate Republican with executive leadership experience. Instead, mired in the fallout of the unpaid babysitters' club, and the helicopter, Swift faced her fate as an unpopular incumbent.

Swift had already declared her intention to run for a full term as governor in the 2002 race when Republican stakeholders, terrified of losing the governorship—the only red prize in a blue state—persuaded Mitt Romney to run. A poll showed Romney a whopping 60 points ahead of her. To win, she would need to make Romney even more unpopular than she was. That meant running a very negative campaign. "I didn't want that to be my legacy," Swift says. It didn't help that Swift would need to raise millions of dollars to get the job done.

"I did get to run as who I was," Swift says, and I think we have a takeaway. Do you! But Swift's glass is as half empty as it is half full. "I wish I could say that there was some great big happy ending to that politically. There's a great happy ending personally. I have three teenage daughters who admire me a lot and I've had a really successful career outside of politics. But it didn't always mean political success to be true to myself."

Former Nevada assemblywoman Lucy Flores knows all too well the promise and peril of being so brazenly one's self. When Flores was elected to the Nevada State Assembly in 2010, she was a young woman in a hurry. One of thirteen children, Flores grew up in a household that struggled with poverty. Her mother left the family when Flores was just nine years old. By the time she was a teen, Flores had joined a gang and spent time in juvenile detention. With the help of a parole officer, Flores slowly turned her life around. She earned a GED, graduated from college, and then graduated from law school.

Flores's upbringing informed her politics and made her especially passionate about education, the school-to-prison pipeline, poverty, and immigration. It also distinguished Flores from her political peers. "What motivated me to service was my experience and challenges. I had a deeper sense of urgency than anybody else," she tells me. That fierce exigency made Flores an appealing public servant. It earned her reelection in 2012 and national buzz as a rising star within the Democratic Party.

But Flores's ferocity had a flip side. She was, she says, the victim of a whisper campaign among political insiders. "I developed this reputation of being difficult to work with, being a bitch, being just impossible. A tyrant."

A 2013 anonymous poll of Nevada legislators, lobbyists, and reporters named Flores "worst Assembly member." Flores says critics used the hardly scientific poll (there were only thirty-five respondents!) as proof of her "bad reputation." During her 2014 race for lieutenant governor, Flores turned the supposed negative into a positive, telling voters she was proud that a handful of lobbyists didn't like her. "It meant I was standing my ground against special interests," Flores says.

In Flores's retrospective analysis, a big part of her reputation stemmed from her unwillingness to fall in line. Politics operate according to as many unsaid rules as those that are stated. Among them: periodically legislators will be asked by party leadership to cast votes to match party priorities that may not match a legislator's own standards or their district's needs. There are those who argue that taking those votes positions you as a good soldier, and enhances your political capital for other things you want to accomplish on behalf of your constituents. And then there are people like Lucy who believe that those votes are a betrayal of their values and their constituents.

"They will pressure you to conform, even if you're not in agreement with that particular policy," Flores says of the party leadership. "I was always willing to say no. Obviously that doesn't sit well when you're in a hierarchical structure where you're supposed to keep your mouth shut and your head down."

Flores knows that she paid a price for being so unabashedly herself. When she ran for a congressional seat in 2016, the Democratic establishment lined up behind another candidate in the primary. But when I ask if, given the chance to do it all over, she'd soften her approach, Flores is adamant that she would not. "Sometimes I wonder, 'Had I been less aggressive and dealt with this sense of urgency, would I still be in office making an impact?' Maybe. But I wouldn't have accomplished what I accomplished had it not been for that sense of urgency."

In 2013, Christine Quinn came within striking distance of making history as the first woman, and first openly gay, mayor of New York City. It was a race that was called "hers to lose." And then she lost.

Part of that defeat was substantive. There were deals that rubbed voters the wrong way, actions that went against a voter referendum, blowback for refusing to support a carriage horse ban. There were also strategic misfortunes. Most notably: a calculation to position herself as Mayor Michael Bloomberg's heir apparent, only to be dubbed the old guard in a change election. Quinn is willing to own that she made mistakes. But almost five years after her searing defeat, there is a personal element to her loss that she is still processing, one that she is generously revisiting at my behest.

"When you're running for office you're craving likeability because it is part of what gets you elected," she tells me. "Who do you want to have a beer with? We know that mantra. We hear it over and over. And we know there's truth to it." Quinn knew she had a likeability challenge, or what her consultants more often described as her not being "accessible" enough.

For wealthy candidates, a claim of inaccessibility might be attributable to their lifestyle. Post-Trump, it is easy to forget that past presidential candidates have struggled with the perception that their wealth made them less like the rest of us, but John Kerry's windsurfing off the coast of Nantucket and Mitt Romney's casually owning a dressage horse rubbed voters the wrong way. Al Gore's seriousness probably made some voters think, "If I were in a social situation with this guy, would I have to pretend to understand carbon emissions?"

Quinn is still trying to figure out exactly what being perceived as inaccessible means for her. "There's this perception of you out there that's kind of amorphous and doesn't feel like you," she tells me. "How do you fix that? It eats away at you."

Some of it wasn't amorphous; it was pretty explicit. Press stories painted Quinn as a sharp-elbowed bureaucrat. A former New York public advocate accused Quinn of berating her, and anonymous "friends and colleagues" described Quinn as "controlling, temperamental and surprisingly volatile, with a habit of hair-trigger eruptions of unchecked, face-to-face wrath."

And then there was the plainly subjective feedback. In a post-election analysis piece for the *New York Times*, writers Jodi Kantor and Kate Taylor examined the gendered response to her candidacy: A Republican candidate said he'd "die" if he had to listen to Quinn's voice for four years. A Brooklyn voter told the *Times* that Quinn was "too masculine." Polling found that Democratic voters with unfavorable views of Quinn described her as "self-interested" and "argumentative."

Quinn contends that some of the press stories were factually inaccurate. But she also concedes that some of the characterizations were an honest reflection of who she truly is.

"Am I tough to work for? Yes. Am I demanding? Yes. Do I sometimes raise my voice? Yes." She pauses, a skilled politician on the pivot. "But am I also extremely supportive of my staff? When I was speaker I had the longest-tenured staff of anyone in city government. Am I as supportive as I am demanding? Yes, I am."

She also faced the same challenge that most women candidates face: be strong enough to be taken seriously, but warm enough to be liked. And for Quinn, being openly gay, there was an added layer to the conversation about just how feminine was feminine enough.

"There was a lot of concern about me not being too woman-y.

Not being too gay. Finding the right balance in my presentation," she explains. "Don't raise your voice. Don't yell. Don't be strident. Don't let them know how tough you are. But don't lean too much into the woman stuff because then people will think you're weak." I ask Quinn how much of the language used to describe her demeanor was simply anti-gay. "A lot," she says candidly. "I think the fact that I'm tough is sexism, but I also think it's 'Look at that tough dyke,'" she says, mimicking the ostensibly unspoken words of her critics. "'Of course *that kind of a woman* yells.'" And then there was the criticism of Quinn's looks: "I was too fat. I looked dumpy. That's a woman thing, but that's also a lesbian thing."

The anti-gay dog whistle politics rose to a painful pitch, if only in Quinn's own ears. Chirlane McCray, Quinn's rival Bill de Blasio's wife, gave a quote to columnist Maureen Dowd about Quinn that was taken out of context. But even with the full context, provided by the de Blasio campaign, it stung: "I don't see her speaking to the concerns of women who have to take care of children at a young age or send them to school and after school, paid sick days, workplace, she is not speaking to any of those issues," McCray—herself bisexual—told Dowd. "What can I say? And she is not accessible, she is not the kind of person that I feel that you can go up and talk to and have a conversation with about those things." *She is not accessible. She is inaccessible.* There it was, again.

The not-so-subtle subtext, the Quinn campaign felt, was this: Christine Quinn is a childless lesbian. How can she possibly relate to a mother? Does she fully qualify as a woman if she has not done all of the things a woman is "expected" to do? Can she really understand your life? The same research that detailed voters' concerns over a woman's ability to be a mother and an elected official found that there is also a penalty for women without children—worry that they will not be able to understand the realities of families with children.

For Quinn and those around her, the dig felt like a calculated attack meant to inoculate the potency of her historic bid. And for all of Quinn's ability to let the insults roll, this was an exception. This was deeply personal.

When Quinn was just sixteen years old she lost her mother to a ten-year struggle with cancer. Quinn's wife, Kim, lost her mother to cancer when she was seventeen. The comment from McCray, however it was intended, felt like a kick in the gut. "Don't make assumptions about why people don't have children," Quinn tells me. "You have no idea unless you've had the kind of painful conversations that goes on between two motherless women deciding whether they want to have children."

There is an irony in this exchange. In answering my query about the secondhand charge of being inaccessible, Quinn becomes the most accessible to me that she will be throughout our interview. She is raw. She is vulnerable. The verve in her voice reveals to me how fiercely protective she is of her wife, of the choices they have made, and of the life they have built together.

Vulnerability is not exactly in Quinn's DNA. She has yet to watch *Hers to Lose*, a documentary that tells the story of the collapse of her campaign. I have watched it and argue that by the end—when it is clear that she will lose—she's more than likeable, she's lovable. "Right, I'm lovable as a loser," she says, and it is clear that she still hasn't grown comfortable with that designation. "All right, I wasn't lovable because I was a loser," she catches herself. "I was lovable because I was vulnerable."

Quinn spent the two years after her loss replaying the race and the moments leading up to it over and over again. She admits that she ran a subpar campaign, for which she takes responsibility. Part of what made it subpar: she didn't run as herself, and lost in the space between too woman-y/not woman-y enough, there are decisions—big and small—that in retrospect feel like mistakes. Quinn is a shoe lover, but when a reporter approached her campaign about running a feature on her collection, the campaign shut it down. "I should have done it because I authentically like shoes," Quinn tells me. "It's not like someone sent me out to get pink faux-croc shoes. I have pink faux-croc shoes. They are a half size too small, but it was a half-priced Jimmy Choo sale! That would have been a good story!"

For Quinn, that is a change brought on by losing: if she runs again, she wants to run as herself. She wants to show off her half size too small, purchased on sale pink faux-croc shoes. She wants to not care. "I am a likeable, kind, fun, warm person. It's hard to get to the point where you can say that and not then apologize for it," she says. "Will people experience me that way? I have no idea. The change is I don't care. There are things I learned about running a better campaign. One part of running a better campaign is that I am going to have fun and be full-on Chris Quinn."

THE POWER OF ALL POWER GRABS

As a journalist, I traveled the country during the 2016 presidential election doing focus groups of millennial voters: Republicans in Iowa who rightly predicted Trump's first place showing, Democrats in New Hampshire who predicted Bernie Sanders's win, Latinos in Nevada, unmarried women in New York, undecided voters in Miami. And in those groups and in every social interaction I had—whether with one of my best friend's aunts, a New Jersey transplant in Boca Raton, or with a diner waitress in Manchester, New Hampshire—top of mind was the question of whether to vote for Hillary or to not vote for Hillary.

No matter where we went or who we spoke with, the argument from those who were anti-Hillary was almost always the same. First voters would detail their case against her: Benghazi, the email server, questionable fund-raising for the Clinton Foundation, or her vote on the Iraq War. Then they'd inevitably downshift to the same final argument: I just don't like her. The subjectivity didn't seem to weaken the argument; it seemed—at least in the eye of the person who was making the case against Hillary—to strengthen it. "Don't argue with me about this," the tone implied. "It's how I feel, and if it's how I feel, if it is in my gut, then there are no objective arguments that can invalidate it."

Even among her supporters, there were often caveats: *Do I think she's perfect? No. I mean, I don't like her, but I'll vote for her.* Supporting Hillary—fervently—was perceived as so socially anomalous that her supporters found themselves quarantined inside Facebook groups like Pantsuit Nation, whispering their support in a safe space.

Oprah Winfrey, a Clinton supporter, even weighed in on this question during an interview with pastor T. D. Jakes: "There really is no choice, people. All the people sitting around talking about they can't decide . . . I hear this all the time," she told the audience. "You get into conversations—and there's not a person in this room who hasn't been in this same conversation— where people say, 'I just don't know if I like her.'" According to Oprah, that was the wrong metric to use. "She's not coming over to your house! You don't have to like her," she proclaimed. "You don't have to like her. Do you like this country? Do you like this country? You better get out there and vote."

The question of Hillary Clinton's likeability dates back to Bill Clinton's 1992 presidential bid. When a rival accused Bill of funneling contracts to his wife's law firm during his tenure as governor of Arkansas, Hillary defended herself. "I suppose I could have stayed home and baked cookies and had teas, but what I decided to do was to fulfill my profession," she said. Most outlets failed to include the latter part of the statement in their readouts: "The work that I have done as a professional, a public advocate, has been aimed . . . to assure that women can make the choices, whether it's full-time career, full-time motherhood, or some combination."

Clinton may have intended the comment as self-defense, but women who had opted out of the professional workforce took the description as a slight. The backlash was intense. "If I ever entertained the idea of voting for Bill Clinton, the smug bitchiness of his wife's comment has nipped that notion in the bud," one voter told *Time* magazine. Hillary spent weeks explaining and apologizing, kicking off a multi-decade effort to make her . . . likeable.

Her likeability, or "favorability" as the question is often positioned in polls, oscillated over the years: down in the wake of Travelgate, up during President Clinton's impeachment, and down again as she departed the White House.

Later, when she was a candidate for senator and then president, the press hyperfocused on Hillary's likeability. In 2008, as she ran for president, a voter asked Clinton how she was dealing with the stress of the campaign. "It's not easy, and I couldn't do it if I just didn't, you know, passionately believe it was the right thing to do," Clinton said, her voice breaking slightly. "You know, I have so many opportunities from this country, I just don't want to see us fall backwards." In an age of reality television, when you can watch a stranger cry about losing a dating competition, Clinton's tears were unusually gripping. People were so shocked by the display of emotion that Clinton basically had to remind folks that she was human. "I actually have emotions," she assured us all afterward. "I know that there are some people who doubt that."

That same year, the question of women candidates' likeability was brought into sharper relief with the emergence of Sarah Palin as John McCain's vice presidential pick. Palin was widely perceived to be affable and charming, but not up to the job. Clinton was perceived to be capable of doing the job, but unlikeable. It was hard to look at "Caribou Barbie" and a woman who had been refashioned into an actual nutcracker and not feel like there's no winning. Especially since they both lost.

As President Obama's secretary of state, Clinton experienced some of her all-time highest popularity. She was largely lauded for her work on the international stage, and reestablished herself as a cultural icon. "Texts from Hillary," an internet meme based on a photograph of Clinton sitting aboard a military aircraft while wearing big black sunglasses and reading from her smartphone, raised the possibility that Clinton was fun, even funny.

When she ran for president in 2016, her favorability dipped, again. In fact, her favorability among Republicans and independents went right back to where it had been during her 2012 presidential race.

When Hillary was acting in the service of her country, people really liked her. Even independents and Republicans held a relatively strong opinion of her while she was secretary of state. But the second Clinton announced her political ambitions, and was perceived as acting in service of herself, those numbers tanked.

"Once I moved from serving someone—a man, the president— to seeking that job on my own, I was once again vulnerable to the barrage of innuendo and negativity and attacks that come with the territory of a woman who is striving to go further," Clinton told writer Rebecca Traister, in a 2016 post-mortem.

The radical act of announcing that she believed she was worthy of service and that she believed she had a chance to run and win immediately made her less likeable. Just like women negotiating for raises or promotions, women are well received when they go to the mat for others; they are punished when they do it for themselves.

Why? Men have power and so it is assumed that it is in their very nature to seek it out and grab for it. By seeking power, they are simply fulfilling their biological destiny. Anyone who has studied war or colonization or watched *The Godfather* understands this. Women, in contrast, are expected to want what is best for everyone. Running for office, aspiring to power, can easily be interpreted as a power grab. For men, running for office is just doing what men do. For women, running violates the cultural expectation that they will act in service to the group. Merely intending to gain power can lead others to believe that a woman is aggressive and selfish, and not as warm and focused on others as she is supposed to be. As Chris Quinn put it, "The day you declare, you will have a new negative."

There's an inherent contradiction in there. Many women are motivated to run for office exactly because they *are* communal and want to better the lives of their neighbors and their peers. But because running for office is such a singular act—it is, after all, one person's name on the ballot—it is often perceived as a selfish act. A woman may run for office from a place of service, but she will more likely be perceived as Claire Underwood or Cersei Lannister, ruthlessly attempting to hoard power for herself.

One study introduced participants to a fictionalized male senator, John Burr, or a fictionalized woman senator, Ann Burr.

Some of the descriptions of John/Ann included this blurb, meant to evoke a power grab:

The Oregon Sun-Sentinel *described [him/her] as "one of the most ambitious politicians in Oregon . . . a politician that has always had a strong will to power." Burr [himself/ herself] has been quoted as saying that "Being hungry is everything . . . it's key to gaining influence in politics."*

Ann Burr paid a price for being ambitious. Voters were less likely to vote for her when her bio included ambition and strong will. John, in contrast, paid no price. In fact, his transparent desire for power made him seem stronger and tougher in the eyes of voters, and thus *more appealing*.

It's not just that people don't like women who seek power; it's that they assume that drive must mean she is devoid of something else. It's strength versus warmth on steroids. The seesaw is perceived to go up on one side, so it is assumed to come down on the other. If she is strong enough to make that power grab, she must lack warmth. In other words: there must be something wrong with her.

Attitudes toward women politicians—about whom as constituents and voters we are encouraged to voice an opinion of—reveal how our culture feels about women leaders at large. There is a bias against women who seek power, women who think they have what it takes to lead, and women who take credit for their success.

What I find illuminating about women candidates and elected officials, especially women who have faced defeat, is that the experience of navigating these expectations has only made them want to be more themselves.

Chris Quinn tempered her truest self in order to win, and

then still lost. But with that loss, she says she learned a powerful lesson. If she runs again, she plans to run as herself, even if that means that people will not like her.

Jane Swift wishes she would have been a little more patient and a little less defensive. But she's not desperately seeking a do-over. When she speaks of her service, she sounds genuinely proud.

Lucy Flores won two elections and lost two elections. She developed a reputation as a fighter, a fierce advocate on behalf of those whose causes she championed, and someone who would always clap back. She'd do it all over again—it's the only way she knows how.

Three days before the 2016 general election, at a Clinton campaign get-out-the-vote rally in Ohio, Beyoncé and pantsuit-clad backup dancers pranced in front of a screen with Clinton's famous cookies-and-tea quote. *I suppose I could have stayed home and baked cookies and had teas, but what I decided to do was to fulfill my profession.* The words, once toxic, had been reclaimed by Queen Bey. It isn't the shattered glass ceiling Clinton imagined, but the reclamation of those words is a reminder that history has the power to revise and redeem.

CHAPTER 6

Public Person; Private Self

This isn't me," I plead, tugging at a black leather motorcycle jacket that a stylist has purchased for me to wear on-air.

I am in the office of Billy Kimball, a writer and producer who is currently the head of programming for Fusion, our young television network. He should be focused on building out a programming slate, but instead he is patiently listening to my grievances.

We are still in the early stages of launching a network, and, having never done this, I naively did not realize how much volatility it would entail. There are so many things we cannot fix: Our multipurpose set is mislit. The control room isn't equipped to render graphics in sync with commentary pieces.

Most alarmingly, we have launched a new cable network just as cable news is on the decline. Our target is millennials, but it turns out my generation isn't watching television. (I should have realized this; my then fiancé and I bought a television and got a cable package for the first time in five years so that I could audit my show each night.) Oh, and in the effort to make me seem young I have been forced into outfits that make me feel like a poser and a dork.

My nightly show is solid, but it's stuck. We're being asked to jazz it up and work around our structural limitations with no additional resources, just sheer will. Since we cannot fix the show it feels like we keep trying to fix the one thing that we have some control over: me. We talk frequently about my hair, my makeup, and what I wear. As someone who wears stretch pants and no makeup in my real life, this is deeply disorienting. But I want to fix what isn't working, and I am beginning to think—based on all this feedback—that what isn't working is me.

My work—part on-air, part off—creates a duality of experience. Behind the scenes, I've encountered the typical office elements of leadership and likeability that come from negotiating, leading teams, and navigating organizational politics. But as a television journalist, I've also grappled with the experience of attempting to be a likeable public persona. It's not enough for my team and network executives to like me. In order to keep my job, I need viewers to like me. I need to be appealing to people who will form an opinion of me based on how I appear and what I say on their television or what I broadcast on their social media platforms. They may not get annoyed with me the way my coworkers do when I pretend not to know how to fix the printer, but viewers might be turned off because they disagree with my analysis or hate my shoes. I'm just as aware of my production assistant's opinion of me as I am of the viewer who keeps leaving voice mails on my answering machine about how my lip gloss looks like WD-40.

And because there is off-TV Alicia Menendez—the person who comes into the office with dark crescents under her eyes, wet hair twisted into a clip, sporting a hoodie—and then on-TV Alicia Menendez (AM), who is always glossy and only needs to be on for forty-five minutes a day, people start to feel free to talk about AM 2.0 with AM 1.0, forgetting that the line between them is less obvious to her than it is to them.

Being a public person can take many forms. You can be a public person in the eyes of the thirty other people in your company, or you can be a public person in the eyes of your 500,000 LinkedIn followers. And having a public platform is increasingly a part of lots of people's jobs. With the rise of social media, there's a fifty-fifty chance your next-door neighbor is an influencer who is doing Instagram posts sponsored by a probiotic brand. It can feel a little like everyone from the trainer at your gym to the fashionista in your office has a following, a fandom, and a Q score. With that democratization of influence, there is increasingly an expectation that high-level professionals will cultivate a public persona. There is incredible pressure to have a look, and a vibe, to be a thought leader on Twitter and a content creator on Instagram. You don't just need to work on your executive presence; you need to work to be omnipresent. That means, for many people, others' opinions of them are based as often on their experience of a larger persona that is pruned and cultivated as they are based on their direct experience of the actual person.

Bobbi Brown, the professional makeup artist and former CCO of her eponymous makeup and skin care line, has managed three brands: Bobbi Brown the woman, Bobbi Brown the cosmetics line, and now Bobbi Brown lifestyle and wellness guru. We may live in an age when regular people nauseatingly refer to themselves as brands, but very few people have had to navigate the legitimate conflation of a person and a thing as Bobbi has. Google "Bobbi Brown" and the first three results are for the makeup, not the person. The complexity of that reality is even more pronounced since Bobbi Brown stepped down from the company in 2016. "My last company has the same name as my birth certificate," Bobbi tells me of disentangling the two.

In 1990, Bobbi was a professional makeup artist struggling to find lipsticks that resembled the color of women's actual lips. At the time, bright, garish hues were all the rage. Bobbi worked with a chemist to create ten natural lipstick shades. They took off. The company was acquired by Estée Lauder and became a billion-dollar brand.

Bobbi describes her teenage self growing up in the suburbs of Chicago as "average" and claims that no one in her high school class would even remember her. But the Bobbi Brown cosmetics line catapulted Bobbi Brown the woman into the spotlight. Suddenly she was *somebody* and everyone seemed to have thoughts on what type of somebody she should be.

During Bobbi's tenure at her cosmetics company, corporate executives decided that the brand needed an overhaul. They hired a consultant to weigh in on the product and on Bobbi herself. She was, after all, the living embodiment of the brand. The consultant told Bobbi that she needed a different wardrobe, and engaged in one of those *Pretty Woman*–style shopping montages. But when Bobbi showed her husband the leather pants she'd been persuaded to buy, he told her what she already felt: she looked ridiculous. Bobbi decided it made no sense to pretend to be someone else. "If I'm going to wear jeans and sneakers in my office, why should I change into heels when I go uptown?" The sneakers became part of Bobbi's signature look, later eliciting compliments from President Obama over her "cool kicks."

Among the other feedback Bobbi has received over the course of her career: *Don't let them know you're a New Jersey soccer mom. Get a pied-à-terre in New York. Make up for your diminutive stature (she's five feet one) by wearing a hat with a feather on it.* (Mind you, said advisor was wearing a hat with a feather on it while delivering this suggestion!)

Just as various forces conspired to make Bobbi something she was not, consultants tried to do the same with the makeup line. They persuaded Bobbi to augment her browns and neutrals with bold, bright colors. But as artists at makeup counters began putting the new shades on customers, they had the same reaction to their faces as Bobbi's husband had to the pants: they looked ridiculous.

Bobbi the brand, just like Bobbi the person, went back to being who it was. As our conversation winds down, Bobbi returns to the tagline of her brand: "Be who you are. You have to be comfortable in your skin," she tells me. And then she offers this reality: "It's too tiring to pretend to be someone I'm not."

For public people, there is often an endless feedback loop. And for women who dare to lead, that feedback often takes the form of direct criticism. So how do you process op-eds about your leadership or questions about your choices without it becoming personal?

"Earlier in my career I worked very hard to be liked, and I took criticism personally," Valerie Jarrett tells me. "As I got older, and my skin toughened, I appreciated that oftentimes people who don't like you don't even know you. We have a tendency to think it's all about us. As I matured, I learned it was really not about us; it's about them."

That outlook served Valerie well during her time as one of the highest-profile figures in the Obama administration:

Public service, which is an extraordinary privilege, comes with a fair amount of criticism. People who are proximate to power, just by definition, are intimidating. When you're in the spot that everybody wants people are going to come after you. That's just the nature of the beast. And I always figured that if I was thinking about why I was there, and I had the confidence of the president, that over time I could win people over. I think if you look at the press I had at the end compared to the press I had at the beginning, I achieved my goal.

The women leaders I spoke with largely echoed these sentiments: Criticism is part of the job. Your skin will toughen. Saddle up. Mari Carmen Aponte, former U.S. ambassador to El Salvador, places value on the lessons learned from an experience rather than evaluating the experience itself. "It will only get better if you get in there, you do the work, you go through processes that are sometimes painful, and learn from it," she told me. "The lesson is what you get out of it, not the experience. If you get into the experience, it becomes very messy and very emotional. But if you look at the lesson, it's much easier to bear."

I write all of this while well aware of two realities. First, most of the women I spoke with who are recognized leaders in their fields are two or three decades older than someone like myself. Putting aside child prodigies and those people who "make it" at thirty, success is generally a slow burn, and given the additional obstacles, an even slower burn for women. I have not spoken with a single woman who learned to care more over time. If anything, realizing that the deck was stacked against them, most women became more comfortable just being themselves. These women have faced down the critics and they have survived. They have hard-earned battle scars. They also have records and accolades they can point to when others doubt them, or when they doubt themselves.

But I also wonder if in addition to being strong and resilient, women who want to lead, especially boomers who had to fight fiercely for basic workplace equality, believe that talking about how much criticism hurts threatens their perception of strength.

I think of Ann Hopkins's case. It was so personal. So public. So highly publicized. If it wasn't humiliating enough to know that Ann's colleagues at Price Waterhouse disliked her so intensely, it must have been mortifying to know that complete strangers were reading about it and talking about it. What does it do to a person's psyche to be publicly derided as universally unlikeable . . . for being you?

At the time, Hopkins argued that she was unfazed by the public criticism. After all, she had spent years in an environment in which she was always the odd woman out. But those close to her told a different story.

"Ann has been crushed by this," one friend told the *New York Times*. "She's been very much hurt by some of the things that Price Waterhouse has said. You have to be cognizant that someone who has had to contain her hurt for many years, as she has, learns not to drop her defenses, to keep her counsel or to make jokes. She's not going to tell you she's cried about it, as she has many times."

When we talk about the price of being a public person, I think of Ann Hopkins bravely saying she was unbothered. I think of Jane Swift refusing to cry in public as she confronted her critics, but weeping privately. I think of public questions about Christine Quinn's identity as a woman who was not a mother opening up old wounds of sorrow and loss. I think of Hillary Clinton, a person we all think we know and wonder: who is she, really, when she gets to be herself?

A PUBLIC PERSON ONLINE

Writer Emily Gould is well acquainted with the perils of being a public person in the internet age. Despite having authored several books, the most lengthy element of her Wikipedia page is the "controversies" section. Among those controversies: back in 2007, as an editor for Gawker, Emily appeared on *Larry King Live* with substitute host Jimmy Kimmel. During the appearance, Gould and Kimmel got into a heated exchange over Gawker's "Celebrity Stalker" feature. The response to Gould's TV appearance was devastating. A clip of the segment got a second life online, where Gould's performance was endlessly mocked and critiqued. Her inbox was inundated with strangers calling her "STUPID" and a "little girl."

The incident caused her to suffer panic attacks, anxiety that a therapist tried to mitigate by reminding Gould that she was not in fact famous. But that's the weird thing about the internet and public consumption, right? Anyone who shares their opinions in public is suddenly a public person. And unlike a pre-Twitter world, where real celebrities might only contend with blowback in daily newspapers or television shows, public people who are much less well known now face feedback 24/7. You wake up in the middle of the night, check your mentions, and there is someone to remind you that you are UGLY, FAT, or STUPID, or, worse, to wish you physical harm.

Given Gould's willingness to continue on in the public sphere despite these blowups, I assumed that she was one of those women who were impervious to criticism. I guessed that she was a person who did not care about being liked. I guessed wrong.

"I had really wanted to believe that I was over the stuff that happened to me in my mid-twenties," Gould tells me. But she wasn't. During the third presidential debate of 2016, the one where Donald Trump loomed behind Hillary Clinton, Gould found herself triggered. "For a month after that I felt physically, emotionally, and mentally taken back to the experience of being publicly humiliated. I was so frustrated with myself because I thought I had done the work to get past this. And I had also thought my experiences had some value. I had suffered in this way but now it couldn't happen anymore. Then to see a powerful and respected woman be humiliated in this incredibly public way made me question everything that I had thought about the value of the work that I do."

Gould understands the opportunities being a public person can create, and the importance of connecting with her readers. At the same time, she knows very intimately the cost of opening herself up for public consumption.

"I feel like I got really lucky that I never became actually famous," she tells me. "That used to be something that I thought that I wanted. Being actually famous seems like hell to me now. It seems like a form of psychological torture, especially for women. There's no way to not be constantly disappointing people and being the subject of so much gendered rage that has nothing to do with you."

Online feedback is . . . confusing. When a public person receives feedback online from followers, they often know very little about who that person is, or if they are a person at all. How much should you care or not care when a random egg is berating you on Twitter?

At the most dangerous and extreme, the feedback one receives via social media can be toxic. More than two in five Americans report experiencing some form of online harassment, with the majority of that harassment occurring via social media. That behavior can take the form of anything from name-calling to physical threats. Men are somewhat more likely than women to be on the receiving end of that harassment, but women are more likely to be sexually harassed online.

A poll by Amnesty International found that one in every five women, across eight countries, had experienced some form of online abuse. That abuse is often violent and sexually explicit in nature. Women with public profiles or, to be more specific, women who dare to voice an opinion, are among the most common recipients of such abuse. For these women, the online feedback loop is less about the oft-discussed appearance of perfection and social comparison, and more often about fundamental physical safety.

All this backlash is especially troublesome when you consider that social media is a women's domain. Women use Facebook more than men, and they lead their male counterparts in Instagram and Snapchat usage by double-digit margins.

Our use of social media means that even if we're not very public people, most of us now experience the dizzying highs and lows of having a version of our lives measured in likes.

WE'VE BECOME THE ALGORITHM

Social media plays right into pressures we have been responding to since adolescence. "Social media rewards behaviors that girls have been long primed to express: pleasing others, seeking feedback, performing and looking good," girl expert and author Rachel Simmons writes in her book *Enough As She Is*. So while the youngest Instagram users play by an entirely different set of rules than we old folk (keeping their numbers of posts low and well curated, deleting posts that don't "perform," and maintaining Finstagrams, or "fake" profiles, that are less curated), many of the women I spoke with feel that social media evokes the same behaviors Simmons ascribes to girls. Women are keenly aware of the feedback loop. When posts perform well, users note the content, and then consciously and subconsciously they produce more of it. Followers liked my recent selfie? Get ready for a million photos of my mug. Sassy subtweet? Guess I need to ignore my dinner companions so that I can reap the rewards of fighting with folks on the internet. What gets rewarded gets replicated.

And just because we're grown doesn't mean that we're all done scrolling through our social feeds keeping track of who is married to a partner who seems like someone we'd also be happy to be married to versus who seems to have an enviable single life filled with girlfriends, pizza, and great apartments filled exclusively with things they chose and not the framed photo of Teddy Roosevelt that my husband won't allow me to give away.

But beyond social comparison, these platforms can feel like yet another dimension of professional comparison. We're not just measuring our results against the person in the adjacent cubicle; we're comparing our following to people who we have decided are vaguely professionally comparable. Who was invited to SXSW? Who launched a new podcast or a new app? Who just opened their own business or their own restaurant? Who delivered a TED Talk? Who was named Employee of the Year (at a company you do not even work for!)?

Those proudly touted career markers can feel like indicators that we are off track, relevant or irrelevant, liked or unliked. We know that social media rarely showcases all the "no's" someone collected along the way, or how their expectation of what an experience would be compared to the actual experience. We saw the Fyre Festival documentaries. We get it. And yet it's so easy to forget.

You've seen all of the studies that say social media is ruining our lives—that we've stopped knowing how to interact with actual people, that we compare ourselves to others, and that doing that is making us depressed and anxious. But the research on social media and mental well-being is inconclusive. Plus, I'm loath to blame social media for an entire generation's self-esteem. I wanted to be invited to cool parties (and then not go) and eat all of those delicious pumpkin pancakes you made yourself—long before Instagram was even a thing. To me, the gross parts of social media are products of a world in which we reward people for showing us an incomplete version of themselves. People have *always* performed themselves and curated an image of their lives; they just did it offline instead of on. All that peer-to-peer comparison was there before, but our universe of peers was much smaller. The difference now that people can "like" our curations is that our likeability feels quantifiable, and thus more easily comparable.

HOW PUBLIC IS TOO PUBLIC?

When Chinae Alexander was a little girl growing up in Texas, she starred as a newscaster in a church play. After the service, as she stood on the church lawn, a man who had been in the pews approached her, dropped to his knees, looked her straight in the eyes, and said, "Little girl, you're going to talk to a lot of people one day." Chinae is not sure that Instagram influence is what that man was envisioning, but it is what has come to pass.

Chinae stumbled into InstaFame after she applied for a social media job at a fitness company. She created an Instagram wellness account as a proof of concept and learned that she had a knack for capturing inspiration in images and words. Since then, she has parlayed her interest in lifestyle, womanhood, and, as she calls it, "badassery," into a large and loyal online following.

I met Chinae in person before I followed her online. In 2016, she was part of a TV segment I taped about single women voters. In person, she was smart, confident, and no-nonsense. The person I first met in real life totally squares with the person I follow on Instagram.

Chinae is often invited to participate in conferences and panel discussions as an expert on social media. Almost every time, she receives a version of this prompt: "You're so authentic. Tell us about being authentic." To Chinae, the question is antithetical to the definition of the word. "Authenticity isn't a trend," she says. "It's not something you *do*. It just *is*. I understand what they're trying to say: Get away from the highlight reel! Get away from this performative lifestyle!" She pauses. "But then we're just teaching people to be performative in a new way." (Side note: Performed authenticity is, for me, one of the greatest crimes of the internet age. I would rather watch someone pretend they are perfect than pretend they are imperfect, or that they are sharing with me a window into their soul when it is nothing more than a ploy to create faux-intimacy that can later be monetized. But I digress . . .)

By showing up as herself—cursing, deriding kale, drinking wine a few hours after spin class—Chinae isn't just authentic; she's relatable. Maybe not to everyone, but to her more than 150,000 followers. With that notoriety, she has become a brand ambassador and found ways to monetize her following.

She is making a living by sharing her life online because she *enjoys* sharing her life online.

MAINTAINING A PRIVATE SELF

This space between the private and the public self, and how likeable or unlikeable those two beings are, feels deeply personal to me. That is because of both my own experience of being a public person and my experience of growing up in a public family. When I was little my dad was the mayor of Union City, our small New Jersey town, then a state legislator. In 1992, when I was nine years old, he was elected to the House of Representatives, and in 2006 he was appointed to the U.S. Senate. My father's celebrity was greatest relative to my place in the world during those years when he was mayor and it felt like everyone knew him, and knew us. Yes, there were gaps between those perceptions and realities—rumors swept the town that my dad owned the iHOP we frequented—but when those perceptions take hold in a one-square-mile town, you might actually have an opportunity to meet people and undo them. When you start to represent 600,000 people, the public persona is what most of them will come to know as "the real you."

Knowing someone intimately—the way you do when you've shared a home, and stomach bugs, and car trips where you scream "are we there yet?" twenty minutes after leaving home—you see how wide the gap can be between how the public perceives a person you love and how you know them to be. Profiles of my dad depict him as tough, and unyielding, which he is. But oftentimes those depictions ascribe motives to that stubbornness that I know to be untrue.

This tension between the public and the private is, as we've discussed, exacerbated for women, and for minorities, because sometimes what is necessary to succeed runs in sharp opposition to what is most authentic to one's self.

In the lead-up to the 2016 campaign, Hillary Clinton seemed to recognize this. She told Diane Sawyer that she was tired of the "likeability" question. "I'm done with that, I'm just done," she said. "I think I have changed, I'm not worried so much about what other people are thinking. . . . I'm going to say what I know, what I believe, and let the chips fall. For me, it's time. I don't know if I could have done it earlier, because I was trying to find my way." The question, of course, still plagued her.

Pundits complain about a lack of authenticity from candidates, but authenticity brings risk. When candidates are fully themselves—raw, dorky, complex—it's more fodder for things not to like. Even if someone is authentically themselves all the time, does that mean we really know them? Not really. We may know the parts of themselves they offer for public consumption. We can assess how much their policies align with their principles. But without spending time with someone can we ever truly *know* them?

In one of my favorite passages in *All the King's Men*, Robert Penn Warren writes, "They say you are not you except in terms of relation to other people. If there weren't any other people there wouldn't be any you because what you do, which is what you are, only has meaning in relation to other people." In an interpersonal sense, this is a mandate to choose those closest to us wisely, to hold close the ones who make us feel most like the version of ourselves we are by ourselves, and to be cautious of those whose presence makes us feel distant from that self. But if we are each only ourselves with ourselves, and then malleable versions of ourselves with others, what does that mean for public people who are consumed by the masses? Do we like who they are or who they purport to be? Do we fall in love with the idea and persona or the actual spirit of a person? Is it possible for any individual to be revealed to us in their complexity through six-minute stump speeches and ninety-second ads?

If you are a public person, likeability takes on new contours. You may be loved by many for the idea of who you are. You will likely be hated by some for your actual truth. Ann Romney, wife of two-time presidential candidate and now U.S. senator Mitt Romney, explained it this way: "The whole thing, with the attacks from everything, you develop—a bubble. From that. A protective bubble. Which you have to do. You have to. Whatever that bubble then projects to somebody is really not what's inside the bubble."

When I ask Chris Quinn if voters will ever allow women candidates to be fully themselves, she gives me this dose of reality: "No one walks around the world being themselves all the time. You'd end up being hospitalized. The world's too tough."

"The [insert name of politician] I know" is a popular public refrain from spouses and children of said politicians. The Mitt Romney I know! The Hillary Clinton I know! The John Kerry I know! Out on the stump, we hear anecdotes from childhood, and glimpses from daily life that are meant to humanize and draw the audience near. Or, in the case of the lauded public figure, to manage expectations. "Barack is very much human," Michelle Obama told *Glamour* magazine of her choice to share intimate details from their domestic life, such as his stinky morning breath and his dirty socks. "So let's not deify him, because what we do is we deify, and then we're ready to chop it down."

These family testimonials, based on years of shared experiences, and the tedium of everyday life—trips to the grocery store and arguing over whose turn it is to take out the trash— remind us what it means to really truly know someone inside and out. As voters, we can talk about who we want to have a beer with the way we discuss which contestant on *The Bachelor* should win the rose. But we don't know who they are when they're walking around in an undershirt, athletic shorts, and dress socks (a deeply unfortunate look that tends to be confusingly popular among the straight male set). We don't know who they are when they process personal tragedy and loss.

I always thought about the authenticity question in a one-dimensional sense: If you're funny in real life, be funny on Twitter! If you wear glasses in real life, wear them on Insta! If you have an accent in real life, speak that way on television!

I now realize that there are more fundamental questions to answer first.

Are you, like Chinae, a person who can share pieces of who you are and not be affected by others' responses to those acts of intimacy? And are you a person who *wants* to share, who *enjoys* the act of sharing? Do you want your public self and your private self to be one and the same?

Or are you someone who *is* affected by others' feedback? Are you sharing out of genuine desire or the expectation that you should? Do you want and need some buffer, some breathing room, between your private and public selves? To be authentic doesn't mean owing anyone other than those you love unfettered access to your full self.

During my conversation with my boss, Billy, that day in his office, he offered me a helpful insight into how to think about this tension. Thank God he is a writer and sees all wacky experiences as future material. It's probably what stopped him from telling me to stop venting and get back to work.

"You don't want to wear the leather jacket, fine," Billy says. "What would you like to wear?"

"If I am being me, then real me would wear a hoodie," I tell him, petulantly daring him to allow athleisure on-air.

He laughs at me, not with me, which is only fair given how ridiculous I'm being.

"Okay, but you're not the real you," he tells me. "Think about it this way: the person on-air every night isn't Alicia Menendez." I give him a quizzical look. "Sure, she looks a lot like Alicia Menendez, and she sounds a lot like Alicia Menendez, but she's not Alicia Menendez."

This is not making me feel any better. I argue that viewers want to see something real, that the best broadcasters are who they are on-air and off. Billy shakes his head in disagreement.

"Do you think Jimmy Fallon would wear a suit every day if he weren't on-air? No. He wears it to show respect to his audience. He wears it to make it feel like a special occasion. That doesn't mean that he's being inauthentic; it means that he's doing his job."

Billy was addressing my surface complaint (self-presenting in a way that felt false), but he was, whether knowingly or unknowingly, addressing my deep angst.

Yes, everyone should be comfortable at work, and everyone should be able to express themselves in a way that is respectful to others, but fundamentally authentic to themselves. I want you to do you. But there also shouldn't be a demand or expectation that every person will offer their full self for public consumption all the time. A gap between the private self and the public self can be easily derided as inauthenticity, but it can just as easily be touted as an act of self-care.

CHAPTER 7

Angry Women Everywhere

I am standing in a conference room in midtown Manhattan, waiting for Carly Fiorina. I'm curious how Carly, as a former CEO of Hewlett-Packard and a 2016 presidential hopeful, has experienced the pressure to be likeable in these various contexts. As I gaze out the wall-to-wall windows, I realize that the building directly next to ours is Trump Tower. Oops. I consider pulling the blinds down and praying that Carly doesn't have a very good sense of Manhattan's geography. After all, a reminder of a competitor who not only triumphed but offended you in the process must taint the view.

When Carly walks in, she is unbothered. She even lets out a genuine laugh. Her skin is thicker than mine.

In a campaign full of explosive moments, a restrained exchange from the 2016 presidential election remains etched on my mind. In the lead-up to the second Republican primary debate, *Rolling Stone* reported that Trump had mocked Carly's looks. "Look at that face," he said offhandedly to a reporter as he watched Carly on television. "Would anyone vote for that? Can you imagine that, the face of our next president?!"

Trump caught flack for the comment. He backpedaled, insisting that he was referring to Fiorina's persona, not her looks. Now, on the national stage, millions of eyes focused on her, Fiorina, the only woman in a sea of ten male candidates, would get a chance to respond. CNN's Jake Tapper, the debate moderator, prompted Fiorina for her thoughts on Trump's remarks, and—lol—*his* persona.

As a producer, I can tell you that the question was designed to create a clippable moment, the kind of exchange that can be played over and over again on cable news and smartphones across America. In the brief pause between Tapper's question and Fiorina's answer, the crowd collectively chuckled. In my own mind, the laughter was followed by the almost faint bumping of fists against tables and chants of "Fight, fight, fight." It was an opportunity for Fiorina to swing back, hard. The question begged for an angry response, or at least an equally immature retort.

That was far from the approach Fiorina took.

Early in her career, Fiorina read a piece of advice about using one's temper that would come in handy in this moment: Use it. Don't lose it. Fiorina's career—rising from a secretary to the CEO of a Fortune 500 company—had provided ample opportunities to test this counsel.

While at AT&T, Fiorina encountered a division manager who needed Fiorina's team to provide him research and support. The manager felt Fiorina's team wasn't delivering fast enough, and on one occasion he was so rough with her staff that he left them in tears. "He was abusive beyond belief," Fiorina tells me. "And most of the people who he was abusing were women."

Carly knew what she needed to do. "I knew what the right thing was. It was to tell him to back off. It was to protect my people," Fiorina tells me. But she also knew that challenging him was a risky move. He was, after all, several levels above her in the corporate structure. He was extremely influential within the company. "I would make an enemy who had a lot of power with people who had a lot of power over my future."

She took the risk. She picked up the phone and told the division manager that he could not make such demands and speak to her staff in an abusive way. Fiorina channeled her anger and spoke to him in what she calls "the language of power." She dropped her voice, demanded that he apologize to the staffers he had upset, and warned that he would not receive the data he was waiting on until said apologies were delivered.

That gamble paid off. The division manager backed off, and the confrontation only improved Fiorina's standing among her employees, and in the company at large. "The people who worked for me thought, 'Oh, she's strong, she's tough, she'll stand up for us, she'll do the right thing,'" Fiorina tells me. "And people always appreciate that." And beyond that immediate boost, there was another lesson. "People knew who this guy was," Fiorina says. "That's so often the case. We all know when someone is terrible. It's just somebody has to stand up and say 'no.'"

That experience also changed Carly's relationship to likeability. "All my life I had worked hard to be liked," Fiorina writes in her first book, *Tough Choices*. "Most of us want to be liked, but I think women feel a special pressure to be pleasant and accommodating. That day I decided that sometimes it's more important to be respected than to be liked."

Pushing back against a bully had undoubtedly prepared her for one of the biggest bullies of all. When Trump's "that face" comment was initially printed, one of Fiorina's staffers called to relay the news. "I laughed and I laughed," Fiorina tells me wryly. "So many men have said so many offensive things about me. It was not the worst thing that's been said about me." Fiorina, as she is known to say, has been called "every B word in the book." In 1982, as sales manager at AT&T, Fiorina's boss introduced her to customers as "our token bimbo." "That face" was just the latest in a long line of sexist comments.

"Donald Trump is an equal-opportunity offender. He insulted everybody in the field. So that's how he chose to insult me. I didn't take it personally," Fiorina says.

This time, Fiorina did not threaten or demand. Her response on the debate stage, elegant, succinct, and controlled, stood in sharp contrast to Trump's petty remarks. "I think women all over this country heard very clearly what Mr. Trump said," Fiorina said to raucous applause. It was a banner moment for Fiorina. While the other candidates struggled to push back against Trump's attacks, Fiorina landed her punch.

When I ask Fiorina how she chose to respond the way she did in that second debate, Fiorina explains her process to me in cool, thoughtful terms. She knew she would be asked to address it, but the line wasn't prepared, and she saw an opportunity to riff off an exchange earlier in the debate between Trump and Jeb Bush.

But that's not what I'm really asking, and so I reframe the question in the bluntest way possible. "How did you not lose your shit?" I ask Fiorina.

"I don't lose my shit very often," she tells me, smiling. "And if I do, it's over personal things like my husband leaving a mess in the kitchen."

You don't have to be a midlevel manager or a woman running for president to contend with workplace situations that might make you angry, whether it's something as consequential as Jerry not turning in his piece of an assignment on time for the fourth week in a row, or Leslie leaving a trail of those damn Cheetos in the break room. And yet a woman who shows anger in a professional setting—whether she is an administrative assistant or an executive—will often be penalized for her anger. Women know this. It's why Fiorina knew going up against her division manager was a calculated risk. An angry woman will be perceived as less competent, and with that she can face real consequences, like how much others believe she deserves to be compensated. That's right: at work, women often pay an actual price for expressing anger.

If the Goldilocks Conundrum finds women choosing between being too hot and too cold, then "anger" is a bowl of porridge served so scaldingly hot that it requires oven mitts. A woman's angry response is immediately chalked up to internal characteristics. In one experiment, researchers Lisa Feldman Barrett and Eliza Bliss-Moreau presented subjects with photos of male and female faces showcasing various expressions. When they asked subjects why each face looked as it did, they found a gender divide. Subjects were more likely to read the female faces as being emotional in response to something internal, a mood swing perhaps. Subjects interpreted the male faces as being responsive to an external situation, something that had been done to them.

Consider what this means for a woman who expresses anger in the workplace: She's out of control. Unhinged. There
is something wrong with her. A man's anger, in contrast, is
presumed to be a reaction to external variables. A frustrating
situation. An unmet expectation. An objective annoyance. As
Feldman Barrett and Bliss-Moreau so poetically summarized
it: "She's a bitch, but he's just having a bad day."

This is especially devastating news for those of us with faces
that aren't naturally friendly or happy. I, for example, have a
serious and unintentionally unfriendly resting face (don't flip
to the book cover to check, I had it fixed in the retouch). It's a
phenomenon called resting bitch face (RBF) or bitchy resting
face (BRF). Writer Jessica Bennett describes RBF as "a face
that, when at ease, is perceived as angry, irritated or simply . . .
expressionless. It's the kind a person may make when thinking
hard about something—or perhaps when they're not thinking
at all." You know it. You've seen it. Think Victoria Beckham or
the Holy Queen of RBF, Kristen Stewart.

There is somewhat of an RBF corollary for men. Research
has found that being baby-faced (having rounded features, a
large forehead, full cheeks) can be a liability for white men
seeking power. Their babylike features mean other people
don't take them as seriously. I mean, *they look like babies*. But
for black men who seek positions of power, that cherub look
can actually be an asset; it can offset the cultural bias that
black men are aggressive or threatening.

While there's little you can do about your face, there is at
least a way to address the anger bias: when women explain *why*
they reacted how they reacted, specifically when they identify
the circumstance that triggered their response, they don't experience the same penalty. So, the next time Jerry is late with
that PowerPoint, as your face flushes and your palms sweat
with rage because you cannot do your job unless Jerry does

his, you might consider explaining to the team, "Hey, guys, I'm pissed . . . BECAUSE JERRY CANNOT GET THE GODDAMN POWERPOINT TOGETHER" or "My blood is boiling because Leslie left 150 calories' worth of cheese sticks on the carpet, someone stepped on them, and now they're caked into the carpet and I know it's going to fall on me to clean up the mess." Maybe *then* people will understand that your anger is externally motivated and, thus, justifiable rather than presuming that you are simply an irrational ticking time bomb.

Here's the real rub: while women are penalized for their anger, men are rewarded. A man's anger makes him seem more competent and more persuasive. In one study, researchers examined the effect of anger in a mock jury deliberation. When the holdout was a man who expressed anger, his show of emotion caused other jurors to significantly second-guess their own conclusions. Men's anger was a powerful tool that made them *more* persuasive. But when the holdout was a woman and she expressed anger, it had the opposite effect; it made other jurors significantly *more certain* of their original verdict. Her anger made her less persuasive.

Women know that anger comes with demerits. Women know that anger makes them less likeable. Women with another marginalized identity know this to be especially true. Women know that an angry woman is seen as a problem woman, even when she is justified in her anger. And women know that while they will be penalized, their male peers will be lauded.

If, like me, you are interested in being an effective communicator, then you're well versed in all the ways that women need to offset the bias against us in our self-expression. You lift your brow to avoid RBF, you uncross your arms, and you smile. You know your aura must exude "namaste" even as the words that come out of your mouth are literally "I am so angry." So, my smiley, singsongy palms-to-the-sky friend, you might likewise find it interesting that this mock jury study was conducted via text. It had nothing to do with the style of a woman's expression, her voice, her face, her body language, or any of the other things she's told are within her control. Participants saw a woman's name (coincidentally, the name they chose was "Alicia"), and even though that woman holdout juror expressed her anger exactly as the man holdout juror expressed his, her fellow jurors wrote her off as overly emotional.

It is tempting to argue that there should be one standard of emotional expression that is applied equally to all. If men get to be jerks in the workplace, then let women do that, too! If men get license to scream and yell, allow women to let it rip! On the other hand, do we really want to use the nexus of male anger and its reward to dictate the universal standard? As much as I envy the response to men's anger, the reward for their perceived passion can also go too far.

Kenia, a political operative, described a man on her workplace's senior management team who used "abusive language, and swearing as a weapon to make situations so uncomfortable that people just wanted to get out of them." Yet he was constantly praised for his aggressive style, and given a pass on the elements that were inappropriate because everyone viewed him as "an effective leader." Is making situations so uncomfortable that people just want to get out of them really what we want leadership to be all about? Shouldn't there be a basic standard of decency that everyone is held to?

Men contend with a variation of this emotion-at-the-workplace challenge. Men who express anger are held in higher esteem than men who express sadness. They are perceived as more competent and deserving of better roles and greater compensation. While an overshow of strength from a woman carries risk, it is an overshow of vulnerability from a man that carries the possibility of social penalty. Both are restrictive. Men's emotions exist in a social hierarchy that also limits how they are able to perform leadership.

Maybe it's time to rethink not just how we penalize women for their anger but how we reward men for theirs.

By the time Fiorina and I rendezvous, Donald Trump is more than a year into his term as president. The face comment, and other comments that were likewise derogatory (and even predatory) toward women—including leaked audio of Trump bragging about grabbing women by their genitalia—didn't register as deal breakers for millions of American voters. Trump's anger was billed as populist and persuasive, and for it, there was no consequence, only a reward.

But if his election exposed the depth of the anger of those who were persuaded by him, it also—depending on who you ask—gave way to or coincided with a cultural reckoning fueled by women who were tired of being quiet and who were ready to express their anger in very real terms. In the initial wake of #MeToo, as the accusations against powerful men mounted and spread, there was a question asked—in soft whispers by some and in booming voices by others: why didn't these women come forward sooner?

It is a question meant to discredit the person who already has less power in the equation. Part of the answer is this: Women know that they pay a price for their anger. Women know that they will face repercussions not just from the person they accuse or expose; there will be blowback from society at large.

Some of the most high-profile revelations of #MeToo—film producer Harvey Weinstein and Fox News anchor Bill O'Reilly—put the question of anger and likeability in sharp relief. On one side were difficult but powerful men who were rewarded for their anger, who became forces to be reckoned with; and on the other were women too afraid to say anything because they knew that their perceived anger would make them less persuasive, less employable, and more disposable. Imagine what would happen if we punished men for their anger and rewarded women for theirs.

OLD RULES; NEW RULES: IS IT TIME TO BREAK ALL THE RULES?

In recent years, there has been a rash of well-intentioned career guides that have aimed to aid women by identifying structural challenges in the workplace and providing tools, tricks, and tips to maneuver around them. As a careerist, I consumed many of those books long before I ever considered writing my own. Whether you too earmarked those guides, or just read the reviews, you know the basic takeaway: the workplace is structurally unsound, but you can still make the most of that shit sandwich by cutting off the crust and adding mustard. I get it: you still need to show up and collect your paycheck even if you are agitating for more radical change. Those books—none more than *Lean In*—have their fair share of critics, including Michelle Obama, who recently said of leaning in, "sometimes that shit doesn't work."

I've read those books from my privileged perch, and to be honest, I got a lot out of them. I found it helpful to consider the role of confidence in what I believe I deserve, and I appreciated the caution against recalibrating ambition in anticipation of the realities of partnership and child rearing. As a person of relative privilege, and a general pragmatist (my husband jokes that I *love* a good "process"), I was comfortable with the premise that women's best options were to navigate and survive systems built and run by white men. The radical-meets-practical promise I took from those books was that if a few women could beat a rigged game and make our way to the top, *then those women* would be in a position to create real, lasting change.

To women with more marginalized identities, with less proximity to power structures, that proposal *never* felt sufficient, and those rules never felt like they applied. And in light of the second wave of the #MeToo movement (an effort first started by activist Tarana Burke and made popular in October 2017 via a viral hashtag) it now seems obvious that that path to change was a bridge to nowhere, littered with booby traps, and even then, only really intended for white women with enough proximity to white men to even entertain the possibility of ascension.

#MeToo hasn't just unmasked a few bad apples; it's revealed entire ecosystems that cultivated those rotten harvests. Much of that revelation has to do with other men, but part of it includes women who aided and abetted them. It has raised questions about what happens when women, in order to maneuver and survive, protect and then act like the men who wrote the rules. Do they ever truly ascend to the top? And when they do, are they conditioned to protect their power by doing more of the same, or are they truly positioned to take the type of risks necessary to shake things up?

As we consider these questions at large, we each turn an eye to our own workplace and own industries: Can we fix these organizations from the inside? Or do they need to be burned down and reimagined? Is the best thing for those of us who can to build our own enterprises, ones where we get to reimagine our respective industries and, with it, workplace culture? How many of us really have the access to capital necessary to do that? How do we find our place in the world when the world is changing so quickly?

While those audacious questions permeate the ether, most of my friends still show up to their nine-to-fives (or in most cases their nine to whenever the work gets done; but don't worry, you can expense an Uber home!) and encounter workplaces that feel relatively unchanged. We as a culture may be bolder on the margins, but how is that trickling down to educated and privileged workers, to say nothing of the women in low-wage jobs who are still agitating for basic protections?

Many of us now realize that we were gaslit into believing that if we tried a little harder or conformed a little more, we could belong. Those who have never had the luxury of even pretending to belong are entitled to roll their eyes at the rest of our naïveté. But I cannot tell you how often I've heard in the course of my interviews with minority women that they too assumed achievement—a degree from Harvard Business School or passing their medical school boards—would buffer them against sexism or racism. It wasn't until they entered new power structures, like VC meetings filled with white men who didn't understand a minority female-focused business pitch, that they fully understood that there is no achievement that fully levels the field.

And yet, as misguided as all the rules that have come before may have been, from the 1950s secretary who was told never to talk about herself to the early 2000s graduate who was told that she should ask for a raise (politely), they created some neat set of expectations. We now realize that driving cross-country with printed AltaVista directions was suboptimal, but we can agree it is better than using a broken GPS.

In this time of great transition, it can feel extra confusing to pick and choose which rules and what advice still serve us and what needs to be abandoned for good. Do we still need the people in charge to like us? Are we supposed to continue to ride the seesaw between warmth and strength? Are we allowed to show up as we are? What if showing up as we are means showing up angry?

We keep being told that the world is changing. Even if that is true, our industries and workplaces will take time to catch up. And in that period between where we were and where we're headed, if it's hard to know which rules apply, it's because the limitations of the old rules have been exposed and the new rules are still being written.

Part II

CHAPTER 8

Addressing the Emotional Cost

As my career has progressed, I've been afforded a number of exciting opportunities to appear on shows that I had once hoped just to see a live taping of, like *The View*, *Real Time with Bill Maher*, and *The Daily Show*. Whenever I was invited on one of these shows, I'd experience excitement that would quickly turn to dread. In the weeks leading up to my appearance I'd obsessively prepare for improbable outcomes. What if Bill Maher asks me to outline the bin Laden family tree? What if Barbara Walters wants me to teach her how to bachata? What if Bill O'Reilly asks if I've ever done drugs? (That last one actually happened.) I'd lose sleep, vomit at least once, and then appear on the show frazzled and mediocre.

In desperate need of fixing, I did the only reasonable thing one could do: I hired a life coach.

Hiring a life coach was not my first foray into coaching. In my mid-twenties, I hit one of many career pivot points. I had gotten into policy work and communications to help people, but my work felt so far removed from the people I hoped to impact that it felt meaningless. I was also starting to worry that I had no hard skills. I could write a press release and a policy paper, but if there were a zombie apocalypse, what actual hard skills would I have to offer? I'm not a doctor. I can't fish or hunt. I don't know how to start a fire. I would be useless and thus one of the first to go.

As a testament to *how soft* my soft skills are, I decided that the answer was to become a life coach. I did some research, and signed up for classes. There were about a dozen of us in the class. I was among the youngest participants. Most participants were in careers in which they felt stuck and uninspired. There were multiple attorneys and at least one former commercial aircraft pilot.

Lots of the theory of coaching centers around the idea that we're whole people—so you can't really coach someone at work without knowing what's happening at home. Each part of our lives is woven into every other part. Even if most of your life feels like it's operating at a 10 out of 10, if you have one element of your life that is way out of whack (say, your health is a 3 out of 10), it's hard to feel the high that you'd expect from everything else.

Coaching differs from therapy in a few ways. Among them, coaching isn't meant to "fix" anything. It is forward-looking and action oriented. You are a coach, not a doctor. Finally, coaching involves powerful questions. Those questions aren't meant to lead, they are intended to prod and to clarify. To allow the person you are coaching to get to their own answers.

As coaching disciples, we spent a lot of time coaching each other. Sitting in a circle of folding chairs under the fluorescent lights of a hotel conference room, we each took a turn being the coach and being coached. When it was my turn to be coached, I felt ready with all the confidence that only someone who is not yet thirty and can't be told shit exudes. I don't remember what we spoke about—my dead-end job? My lack of fulfillment? What I do remember is that as the student coach poked and prodded, I began to get defensive. My guard went up. I could feel my shoulders inching toward my ears. And then, try as I might, waterworks poured down the front of my face. I wanted to tell the fellow student coaching me to back off. I wanted the questions she was asking to say something about her, but my response to the answers said everything about me. The surprise to the room wasn't about how aggressive she had been; it was around how vulnerable I had been. Others in the room agreed that there was a dissonance between what I projected and what I felt inside. So much blustery confidence, so much less deeply held self-esteem. So much fight but, really, so much heart.

The roots were obvious enough: I was a sensitive kid whom everyone tried to prepare for the real world by telling her to be less sensitive. I was a crier who everyone worried would cry at the wrong moment and get her ass kicked, either figuratively or literally. I had learned that my softness was a liability, something that could get me hurt, and so I buried it and learned to rely instead on the part of me that was unflappable and tough.

Over the course of the next few sessions, we all did a lot of crying, and most of us realized that we needed coaching more than we needed to coach others. As others entered the phase of signing up for level 2 and naming their future coaching businesses, I realized that I had gotten what I needed out of the course. I did know what I wanted to do: I wanted to help people lead empowered, informed, happy, healthy lives, but I didn't want to do it through one-on-one coaching. I wanted to do it through media. That part gave me tremendous clarity.

The other part, my true self, would take more time. A new self was revealed to me, and I was not willing to embrace it. Change—real change—is hard. So I put myself back together more or less as I had been before, and continued through the world as best I knew how. I am not talking about a conscious choice to have a public self, separate from a private self, where one is choosing what to share and with whom, out of discretion. I'm talking about straight up not knowing who you are when you're not responding to others' ideas of who you ought to be.

By the time I came back to coaching years later, post–live television performance anxiety, I was reconfronting the previously identified but unremedied misalignment. Together my coach Ileana and I got to the source of what was holding me back: a preoccupation with being liked, a fixation on a thing I cannot control.

I hoped identifying the source of the problem would fix the problem itself. Just as a nerdy girl in an eighties movie gets a five-minute makeover and learns she's basically a model, I assumed that I would do some breathing exercises and emerge confident AF. But it turns out unlearning thirty years of lies you've told yourself about who you are and who other people expect you to be takes more than a few sessions with a trained professional.

In my case, addressing the internalized cost of the demands of likeability required admitting that I cared what others thought of me, and not to anyone else, but to myself. Part of that acknowledgment meant examining the conditioning I, like so many women, received from a young age. It will come as a surprise to no one that I was that "bossy" girl, with her hand constantly in the air, who was told early and often that I needed to tone it down and hem it in. I had great parents who cultivated self-esteem and encouraged me to strive and compete, and still, all of the external messages infiltrated. I cared about pleasing my friends. I cared about pleasing my teachers. I wanted the gold star not only of achievement, but of acceptance.

I worried what others thought of me and I was willing to make concessions to guarantee a positive response. And when I stuck to my guns and acted like myself, I often had late-breaking anxiety and remorse for not being more contained. I am a very sensitive person, and would likely have been very aware of others' feelings, but social conditioning put that awareness into overdrive.

It took me a long time to admit that I care. It feels so . . . pathetic. But once I admitted it, and processed it, I turned my attention to this question of likeability. What followed was months of learning how my own obsession with being like-able was my kryptonite. On-air, I was so terrified of saying or doing something wrong that I'd default into my survival mechanism, hiding behind my intellect, rather than allowing myself to be vulnerable and warm. The irony, of course, is that like pretty much everyone, who I really am is more appealing than who I pretend to be when I feel threatened or unsure. In my personal life, I began to realize how once I was free to be myself, I only wanted to be with people who allowed that person to show up.

Being ourselves and becoming ourselves are processes that, if we are lucky, are constant and evolving. The challenge for those of us who care about how others think of us and those of us who have spent a lot of time in environments that have required us to culturally adapt is that in the process of being and becoming, we've likely taken some cues that did not fully serve us. And so like anyone who has put the wrong address in Waze, we've arrived at a new self only to realize it was an error, realized that we needed to retrace the steps that got us there, and then kicked ourselves because we now worry that we'll be late to arrive at our actual intended destination. Sometimes we worry that we'll never get there, that we'll just keep dashing between exits on the New Jersey Turnpike for the rest of our lives, always coming and going but never arriving.

Most of our discourse around women and work understandably focuses on the tangible costs of gender bias, like lost wages and missed opportunities. But the cultural bias that women should care what others think of them, and the narrow space they are given to exist as likeable persons, much less likeable leaders, hits more than just their wallet. The emotional cost is steep.

RUMINATION

I have an overactive imagination. As a little kid, I decided that my grandmother should marry Mr. Belvedere, the fictional British housekeeper from the sitcom of the same name. If they were married, I reasoned, surely he'd come to my house to cook and clean. This creative mind, matched with my sensitivity toward others, can be hazardous. If texts from a friend are not returned, I worry that I have said something wrong and I can come up with at least a dozen things that can possibly be, dating back to the advent of the friendship. If invites are not extended, I become convinced that I have alienated everyone . . . even if I did not want to go in the first place.

The problem is that for someone like me, thinking about others quickly becomes *overthinking* about others. The late Yale professor Susan Nolen-Hoeksema put a name to my favorite pastime: rumination. She claimed that women were "suffering from an epidemic of *overthinking*," tying the behavior to increased rates of depression and anxiety.

Any overthinker knows the logic behind rumination well: if you can just think about something enough, swirl it around in your mind like a fine wine, surely you will find a solution or a truth, or at least a note of tobacco. Only in reality, the opposite is true: questions don't lead to answers; questions lead to more questions. *I told Paola that I was going to miss her birthday dinner because I'd be traveling for work. Then she said, "It's okay!" but didn't add an "xo." Is Paola mad at me? Does she think I'm selfish? Am I selfish? Is this why I had no friends in seventh grade? Or was it because I was lactose intolerant and hadn't figured it out yet?*

This is what Nolen-Hoeksema called "the yeast effect." The questions start with a specific event, but quickly lead to larger questions about yourself. And, because women are more likely than men to define themselves by their relationships to others, this "excessive relational focus" can provide ample material for the ruminator.

Maintaining a healthy relationship to likeability requires knowing that likeability is an outcome that cannot be guaranteed. Let me say that again: likeability cannot be guaranteed. Once you start believing that how someone feels about you absolutely *means something* about you, once it has you doubting yourself, it is time to put your hands up, step away from the questions, and give yourself room to breathe. Playing the exchange over in your mind isn't making you more likeable and it's not getting you closer to an answer; it is wasting your time and leaving you out of sorts.

THE REAL SELF AND THE IDEAL SELF

Let me tell you about my ideal self. She remembers people's birthdays. She sends birthday cards. On time. With lovely penmanship. Karen Horney, a German psychoanalyst, theorized that in our attempts to strive toward an ideal self, many of us create rules of what we should do and who we should be. The shoulds, theoretically, bring us closer to our ideal self. She dubbed this striving "The Tyranny of the Shoulds." That tyranny can take many forms. *I should do my hair before I go out. I should wear earrings. I should visit my grandmother. I should make more money. I should go to church. I should go to the gym. I should get married. I should have a baby. I should learn to speak Mandarin. I should be a better friend. I should return that call. I should clean out my inbox. I should stop writing these down because they are stressing me out.*

For certain personality types—the type A's, the good girls—it's easy to "should" your life away. None of us are free of obligations, and there will always be things we feel obligated to do (and let's be honest, there are "shoulds," like brushing your teeth, that are on the list for a reason). But if one's major life choices are dictated entirely by what one should do, what is expected, rather than what is authentic to one's self, it would seem impossible to live a happy, self-actualized life. The person who gets married only because she feels she "should" is likely not entering a happy union. The person who pursues a high-paying job only because she believes she "should" will likely find that satisfaction fleeting.

At work the "shoulds" can be more nebulous. Should you respond to your boss's 3 a.m. email at a lightning clip? Should you go to an after-hours work event even though you want to go home and cuddle your dog? These questions are hard to answer without more context. You're enjoying your weekend and a colleague emails you. For a people pleaser, there is a tendency not just to want to respond immediately for the sake of efficiency but to be well regarded by that peer.

I suspect that for many of us, the space between our real

self and our ideal self is drawn not just by our aspirations to be better, but by some sense that our ideal self would be better regarded than our real self. I'm a big proponent of self-improvement, but if you're governed by what you should do, how do you ever get a chance to be? If you're always striving toward your ideal self, does anyone get to know the real you, the one who is here, right now?

Anyone who has been told they need to change over and over again might make so many concessions along the way that once they're ready to be their authentic selves they have no idea who that is. Your authentic self feels like a thing you should know at a visceral level, but if you paper over it enough times, eventually you have to do the hard work of excavating the remains.

A NOTE TO MY FELLOW CARERS: LEARNING NOT TO INTERNALIZE OTHERS' OPINIONS IS A PROCESS

If you care what others think about you, and I have convinced you that you are paying a price for that care, you may, as I have done, try to care less. But then, inevitably, you will relapse into caring. Someone will say something wrong in a meeting and you'll hesitate to correct them. A friend will ask for your honest opinion, but you know that your honesty will be alienating. Or you'll stand up for yourself, you'll get what you need, you'll be proud of yourself . . . and then you'll worry that standing up for yourself has made you difficult and unlikeable.

All of a sudden there is that flush of recognition: you care. Then comes the second flush: you care, you know you are paying a price for caring, so you get annoyed with yourself for caring. You are unlikeable to yourself because you want to care less about being liked but you can't totally get there. You made rules for yourself, then you broke them. You have no self-control. You are destined to a life of preoccupation with others' opinions of you. That rabbit hole is dark and deep.

So here's the thing: if you are trying not to internalize others' opinions, and you find yourself doing it anyway, that's okay. That's part of the process of disentangling all these expectations and learned behaviors.

Years ago, I acknowledged how much my obsession with likeability was costing me, and I made the choice to care less. And every day since, I have cared. I have cared so much. Yes, I have put it in perspective, I have noticed my own triggers, and my own defaults, but the desire to be well regarded is still there.

It takes a long time to actively break up thought patterns that you've spent years developing. You have to interrupt those patterns again and again, building your ability to put your needs and your wants above what is most immediately pleasing to others.

Caring *too much* about being well liked carries too great a cost: your time, and your mental and physical health. Ruminating can keep you very busy! It's exhausting, and unproductive, not to mention depression and anxiety producing. Striving for an ideal self makes it really challenging to enjoy the self you already have. And, at the risk of getting too meta, being annoyed with yourself for not being able to quit likeability cold turkey just reinforces all the self-loathing that we're trying to free ourselves from in the first place. Plus, all of these behaviors take us further away from our true, authentic selves. They set us up to be forever in hot pursuit of something so elusive that we're never able to just be.

WHAT YOU CAN DO FOR YOU

Against the backdrop of my reimagined world, I realize that women are reading this on the train to their job in the real, current world, where they want a raise, and a promotion, and want to be seen as a leader. There is plenty of literature dedicated to how to get those things while the world is the way it is. But beyond those necessary skills, I want to offer you strategies and realities that relate specifically to the internal cost of tension between likeability and success.

Take Care of You

Self-care can be a hot bath and a face mask, but it can also be the daily work of reminding yourself that—whether you care or don't care—what others think of you is not the sum of who you are. Be kind to yourself and take care of yourself so that you can sort through all the feedback you receive in a way that is constructive and productive. It's hard to know what is objective and what is subjective, what is advice that is worth taking and worth discarding when you're already doubting yourself.

"The world will always supply enough critics, so do not be your own worst critic," Arianna Huffington counsels. "That's when we're most likely to doubt ourselves and most likely to hold back and not speak our minds. This means dealing with the voice I call the obnoxious roommate living in our head, the voice that feeds on putting us down and strengthening our insecurities and doubts. We all live with that voice, but the times it comes out the most is when we're tired, stressed, and run down. That's when we're most likely to doubt ourselves, most likely to react emotionally, and when our perceptions are at their shakiest."

The more you identify with your authentic self, give yourself time and space away from work, and surround yourself with people who allow you to be that self, the easier this will all be. Thinking so much about how complicated it is to reject likeability in the workplace has had a strange effect on me: it's liberated me to care less in my "real" life. Here's what I mean:

work, especially work as a public person, will always require an element of performance. So how much of our lives will we spend "performing" a version of ourselves? I considered crunching these numbers, but I burned my TI-83 calculator in effigy a long time ago.

As Annie Dillard famously wrote, "How we spend our days is, of course, how we spend our lives." So if you spend anywhere from a fifth to a third of your life at work, and you can't be totally yourself at work, does that mean you spend a minimum of a fifth of your life being not yourself? I don't want to fuel your existential angst, but that sounds pretty terrible.

If you're already giving up a good chunk of your life to modulating your strength and your warmth, policing your anger, and you want to live an authentic life—one that is aligned with your priorities, your values, and your very essence—then why would you give up another second being anything but your truest self in the rest of your life?

Push for More Subjective, Concrete Feedback

When executive coach Caterina Kostoula's clients receive critical subjective feedback, she encourages them to ask two questions. The first is to ask for evidence of how these qualities are impacting their work or their team. I ask Caterina how one can request "evidence" without sounding like they are re-enacting a court scene from *Law & Order.* Caterina suggests asking, "Can you be more concrete?" or "How does this thing I do impact my work?" In some cases, the inquiry allows the reviewer to offer more helpful, objective feedback. In other cases, it forces them to reconsider the necessity of the commentary.

Another tactic Caterina recommends: when being told one is aggressive, for example, ask, "Compared to whom?" This again forces the reviewer to consider their feedback in the context of unconscious biases they may hold. The feedback may still apply, but these questions will help inform how you proceed.

Find Your People

Navigating all of these external and internal challenges is much easier when you don't have to do it alone, and you are more likely to feel you belong in your workplace when you are in community with others. Many workplaces have employee resource groups, communities within communities, voluntary groups, led by employees, that are intended to create a sense of belonging for individuals with shared identities or life experiences. These are places where workers should feel safe and encouraged, where they can talk about challenges unique to their experience, and suss out what's working and what's not working and seek out solutions.

Having never worked in a workplace that actually had these groups, I, like many women, have built my own cadre of professional peers whom I rely on for gut checks, recommendations, and counsel. I was recently in the studio for a recording of *Latina to Latina*, the podcast I host and co-own with our executive producer, Juleyka Lantigua-Williams, when a request came through via email asking me to moderate a panel. In order to do it, I would have to travel. I would be away from my daughter for two days, and the event organizers were not offering compensation. My gut told me it wasn't worth the sacrifice, but I worried that saying no would jeopardize future opportunities. I took the question to the other two working moms with me in studio, Juleyka and our guest, author Carmen Rita Wong. They both said "pass" without skipping a beat. Not only did they give me sage advice, but they buoyed me so that I didn't once doubt my decision.

There have also been times when these peers have told me I need to reconsider my approach or called out legitimate, substantive areas of improvement. Their insights on how I can stretch and grow are among the most useful. Their honesty and perspective are everything.

Finding your people gives you space to do you, to strategize, and, most important, to feel a little less alone.

Find a Sponsor

For the longest time, mentorship was the hottest professional ticket in town. It was as though a person who could give you the right advice and counsel was all that stood between you and the career of your dreams. Mentorship can be a many-splendored thing—it is valuable to have the perspective of someone who roots for you and can offer tough love or a gentle nudge. A truly valuable mentor is able to help you identify and articulate your strengths and your goals. They help you navigate the unwritten rules of the organization or industry you are seeking to summit. This type of guide is particularly important for women and minority workers.

But advice takes you only so far; at some point, you need action. Enter a professional sponsor. In her book *Forget a Mentor, Find a Sponsor*, economist Sylvia Ann Hewlett makes a compelling case for sponsorship.

Here's the primary difference between a mentor and a sponsor, per Hewlett: a sponsor delivers. They make you known to power players inside and outside of your organization, they advocate for your promotions and pay raises, and they connect you with opportunities for improvement and advancement.

Hewlett also argues that in addition to the very tangible aforementioned elements of sponsorship, and the hopeful positive outcomes, sponsors provide cover for their protégés. This is particularly interesting to me, because that cover can apply to many of the likeability traps we've discussed. If a sponsor is telling others how amazing a woman is and how much she's accomplished, it lessens the burden on that woman to contend with the tension between taking credit and being well liked. If there are others inside the organization who fret that a female employee is too much or too little, a sponsor can reframe or simply shut it down. A sponsor can advocate for you because they know how hard it is for you to advocate for yourself.

To find a sponsor, Hewlett recommends considering individuals within your organization or industry who, "(1) are already aware of your skills and strengths, (2) stand to benefit from your help, and (3) have the clout to move you toward your goal." Once you've identified someone who might be a good fit, get in front of them. That can take many forms, such as requesting a meeting or approaching them at a networking event. Once you have their attention, you have to offer them something useful in exchange. It can be a potential collaboration, or insights you can offer in return for the specific type of advocacy you are hoping for.

If that person isn't game, ask if they know someone else who might be a good fit. Then ask for an introduction to that person. (Hi, my fellow guessers. I know this is making your hands sweat. This will not be easy, but it will be worth it.)

In targeting a would-be sponsor (should you be lucky enough to have a choice!), do not yourself fall into the trap of choosing someone whom you like or who shares your style. In fact, some of the best sponsors are people whose styles are different than your own. You're not looking for a new best friend; you're looking for someone who has interests that align with yours, power, a big network, and a willingness to use those assets on your behalf.

And remember, this is a reciprocal relationship! Once you find a sponsor who is a fit, give as much if not more than you receive. Constantly deliver excellent results so that you make your sponsor look good in the eyes of everyone they introduce and tout you to. Look for opportunities to provide your sponsor with industry insights and information. Make their investment feel worthwhile.

Know When It Is Time to Leave

Nicole went to a top-tier law school and then joined one of the best law firms in the country. She liked the work, her coworkers, and the firm itself. But as a midyear there was an incident that changed Nicole's outlook. She was assigned to work on a team helmed by a senior associate, Mark, who was a few months up from his partnership vote. According to Nicole, he was a bad manager, quick to lash out at others and assault his team with torrents of emails.

One evening, Nicole and another female associate left the office to attend a firm-sponsored women's event. During the dinner, a court handed down an unfavorable decision—one that had ramifications for all the team's other cases. As soon as Nicole and her colleague saw the rapid-fire exchange that had transpired in their absence, Nicole emailed Mark and explained that she and the other female associate were leaving the women's event to head back to the office.

"Women's event?" Mark responded via email. "Tomorrow, Steve and I are going to have a white male event."

Nicole was stunned. Hadn't the firm asked her to attend this event? Why was her manager insinuating that she wasn't working? And why would he undercut the need for professional support among women attorneys when the profession had trouble retaining them? She gave herself a minute to consider whether her indignation was justified. She decided she couldn't let it slide and responded to Mark's "white male event" remark with "Why? That's every day."

Mark doubled down, responding, "Oh because you women are so discriminated against."

Nicole was fuming. And as much as she was insulted, she realized that the exchange and the resentments underlying it could have big consequences. "This is not some guy who sits down the hall from me," Nicole explains. "This is my boss. He's the one who writes my reviews."

Nicole reported the exchange and the firm removed her from Mark's team. Managers had what they described as stern discussions with Mark, but by Nicole's standards there weren't any real repercussions. In fact, a few months later, Mark became a partner.

At that point, Nicole wanted to leave the firm. To her, Mark's promotion, along with a series of other decisions about partnerships, telegraphed the firm's true values. But then, she had her doubts. She had, after all, been on this path for seven years. Part of her reticence to quit stemmed from how much of her identity was wrapped up in her professional life. "I was a lawyer. I was working at this firm. It was who I was," she explains. And then, there was the fear about what others would think. "There is an understanding that if you leave in your seventh or eighth year it's probably because you're told you don't have a future as a partner at the firm," Nicole explains. "There was a part of me that was worried that if I left it would be signaling to the world that I hadn't been successful. I thought everybody would judge me, myself maybe the most." So she stayed.

Two years later, in her annual review, Nicole's managers told her that she was on track to make partner during the next round of votes. She didn't know if she wanted to become a partner, but the proclamation was validation of her hard work and commitment. Nicole's managers also told her that she would receive additional feedback prior to the partner vote only if she solicited it.

Shortly after her review, a senior male partner who had never worked directly with Nicole requested that she be put on one of his cases in advance of the vote. Nicole did what she always did: she was pleasant and diligent, and she pushed back when she disagreed. But soon after Nicole joined the case, two of her managers offered her some unsolicited feedback, the type of feedback they told her *not* to expect. The managers claimed they were doing the same with all of the senior associates who were up for partner, but when Nicole asked her peers if they had similar conversations, none had.

The assessment came from the senior male partner, through Nicole's managers. "There is a perception that you are passive," they told her.

Nicole was stunned. "I'm already on the defensive because that's an alarm ringing bell for me as an Asian-American female." In her entire time at the firm, in all of her annual reviews, no one had ever described Nicole as passive. In fact, understanding this bias against Asian-American women, Nicole had conditioned herself to speak up in every meeting she was ever in.

"It is not at all substantive," Nicole's manager assured her. "And it's not a communications issue. You're a very strong communicator." The advice was this: "Go to the partner's office, seek him out, treat him like a client. Let him know that his case is the most important."

"*Make him like you,*" they told Nicole.

Here is what Nicole wanted to say: "The problem is this guy's perception, but it's my job to fix it. Why is it my job to make everyone feel better? To meet them more than halfway? This guy doesn't realize he has unconscious bias. Who is telling *him* to address *that*? How are you helping *him* change? How are you making the place get better? You can't be shocked when things get worse instead of better when you sweep everything under the rug. You make me talk on panels and at recruiting events about being an Asian-American woman at this firm.

It's just preposterous to me that on the eve of the partnership decision this is the feedback you give me."

Instead, Nicole thanked her managers, closed her door, and cried in the privacy of her office.

For a week, she mulled it over. She considered "sucking up." But the more she thought about it, the less palatable it seemed. There had been the incident with Mark, the firm's inadequate response, and now a senior partner threatening to derail Nicole's path to partnership over a racially biased perception. To make matters worse, her strongest advocates were allowing it to happen.

Nicole was so angry, so tired of playing on someone's else terms, so sick of the hypocrisy that she quit.

I want you to consider how dramatic that decision must have been. This is a people pleaser who endured three years of law school. One year clerking. Seven years at the firm. All presumably leading up to becoming partner. And just as she was on the precipice of the very thing she was building toward, she decided she was done. For Nicole, refusing to do what she was told she'd need to do in order to ascend, quitting and quietly vacating her office was extreme. It was also liberating.

"It was the first time in a long time, or maybe ever, that I was really like, 'I don't really care at all. I don't care what anybody thinks,'" she says.

By her estimations, Nicole did everything right. Not only did she do the work, deliver results, and behave pleasantly, but she consciously countered bias at every turn. She spoke up. She threaded the needle between competence and warmth. She acted like more than a worker bee, but somehow avoided being dubbed a dragon lady.

But even that was not enough.

First, Nicole contended with explicit bias—a manager's snarling commentary about a women's networking event.

"Tomorrow, Steve and I are having a white male event" is the type of out-of-touch remark that only serves to reinforce the importance of networking to women who are navigating the lonely experience of working in majority-white, majority-male spaces. And then this little spoonful of sugar that did not help the medicine go down: "Oh because you women are so discriminated against." In that remark, there is so much to unpack: Women are complainers. Women are hysterical. Women are drinking Chardonnay at a fancy party while we men are busy doing the real work.

Then there was the issue that anyone who has ever contended with workplace discrimination will recognize, the same issue that Adaora encountered: by addressing a problem, the person who has been discriminated against runs the risk of becoming the problem.

Finally, Nicole did everything she was asked to do, until she was told that a fully subjective and false claim against her threatened her partnership. She was told that what stood between her and the job she had long strived for was someone else's impression of her, an impression that underscored the racial and gender bias against women like Nicole.

"*Make him like you*," they told her.

No wonder she was done.

Nicole will be the first to admit how incredibly privileged she is to have had the financial security to quit her high-paying job. Most people, including those who have experienced equally or more egregious transgressions in the workplace, cannot afford to walk out the door. But how many of us who could leave instead choose to stay, not even looking for something that is a better fit, long after we've seen the writing on the wall?

Sometimes it's not the organization you're a part of that isn't the right fit, it's just the team. Look for opportunities to reposition yourself within the existing structure. Sometimes it's a rough patch, a project or a manager with which we don't align. We can survive that if we know there is a light at the end of the tunnel. But sometimes an organization like Nicole's shows us over and over again that they do not value who we are and the skills we offer. When that happens, it's time to make an exit plan.

Beyond her economic and educational privilege, do you know why Nicole could leave? Because she knew her worth. She knew she was smart, hardworking, and a joy to work with. While she had her doubts about how others would perceive her decision to leave, she never doubted her own ability. She knew she could find better opportunities in part because she owned that she was *worthy* of those opportunities.

About a year after her departure, a partner at the firm lamented to Nicole's husband that she had chosen to leave. "She was beloved," he said with a sigh. But Nicole didn't want to be loved, she wanted to be valued, and treated as if the firm understood her worth as well as she did.

Find Opportunities and Workplaces That Align with Your Skills and Style . . . Even If That Means Building That Place Yourself

The women I spoke with who were happiest work or have worked in organizations where their skills, their unique talents, and their style are valued. The others who expressed the greatest levels of happiness were those who had struck out on their own. Alexandra Wilkis Wilson and Anna Harman are examples of both courses.

Alexandra is a serial entrepreneur, which means that most of the organizations she's been a part of are opportunities and environments of her own creation. She is an innovator and a dealmaker with an unbelievable track record of building businesses and creating brands. She's also one of the kindest people I've ever met.

Alexandra cares about being well liked. She's the type of person who had sixteen bridesmaids in her wedding party and, ten years later, still worries that she might have hurt feelings by leaving friends out. But beyond her natural demeanor, Alexandra is a believer in the power of likeability. As an entrepreneur, it's played a role in her relationship with everyone from cofounders and early team members, to employees, to investors. "You don't need to be best friends with them," she says with a laugh, "but there has to be something about you—your personality, your vision, your work ethic—that attracts them. In start-ups, people work really long hours, it might never be lucrative, and it certainly isn't lucrative in the beginning. You have to believe in the people, in the team, and in the long-term vision."

In meetings and among peers, Alexandra is a peacemaker. "I like harmony," Alexandra tells me, a little sheepishly. "When I see two people disagreeing on something—I feel like it's my job to make peace. I try to rephrase things so that people's feelings aren't hurt, and so that one person can see the other person's point of view." It's been more than a decade since Alexandra launched her first start-up, Gilt. In that time, she has gotten better at delivering tough messages, but she admits, "I never like doing it."

In 2016, as Alexandra prepared to launch Fitz, an in-home wardrobe styling service, she hired Anna Harman to be the start-up's head of operations. On paper, the two women are similar: both grew up in New York, and both are bright, ambitious, and well educated. But likeability for Anna was never top of mind. In fact, when I ask Anna about likeability, her response is "I've literally never thought about this."

After graduating from college, Anna went to law school, practiced law, and then spent two years working at Bridgewater Associates, the world's largest hedge fund. Bridgewater is known for a workplace culture of "radical transparency." It has been called "the world's largest and indisputably weirdest hedge fund," a "cauldron of fear and intimidation," and "unusual and confrontational." Just thinking about it makes my hands sweat. Anna, by contrast, thrived there.

In some ways, Anna's work experience feels anomalous. She is an unapologetically assertive professional woman who feels that she has never been penalized for being tough. If anything, her manner has been lauded everywhere she has worked, and she has been rewarded for her contributions. Part of that stems from the fact that Anna has always been drawn to workplaces that align with her priorities and her style. If, in an interview with a potential employer, Anna feels the tiniest hint that it is not a fit, she won't consider the opportunity.

And beyond choosing opportunities and institutions where her unique skill sets will be valued, Anna sees confrontation as a constructive rather than destructive act.

"I am a very transparent, honest, direct person. I'm also very genuine and very loyal. I really want to build deep relationships with the people in my life," Anna says. "As a function of that, there have been times where I've had to make professional choices that many people would think are really hard things to do." Anna lists examples: offering tough feedback, organizing a team, firing employees. "I've been very close friends with the people that I'm working with but I've had to tell people, 'You did a really bad job on that' or 'You really could have done a lot better,'" Anna explains. "The thing that I've thought about in that situation is—how can you make it the most productive and the most positive experience that it can be? If someone's not doing well in their role at work, they're probably more stressed out about it than you as their manager are."

Coming from Bridgewater, the start-up environment at Fitz was a big departure from what Anna was accustomed to. "Anna found our culture completely warm and fuzzy," Alexandra says with a smile. One might imagine Alexandra's and Anna's opposite styles would put them on a collision course: the peacemaker versus the confrontationist. In reality, each complemented the other. "Anna was the yin to my yang," Alexandra tells me. "I warmed her up, and she toughened me up." "I wanted to work with someone who could be complementary to me," Anna says. "Much of Fitz's success commercially is attributable to Alexandra, and much of Fitz's success operationally is attributable to me. We were able to divide and conquer."

"Get Out of Line"

I recognize that leaving a job as Nicole did, finding a series of aligned workplaces as Anna did, or founding your own businesses, as Alexandra did, can all feel like distant ideals. There may be a wide gulf between those aspirations and your current reality.

In that space, I offer you this counsel from Juleyka Lantigua-Williams, the joint owner and executive producer of our podcast, and the CEO and founder of Lantigua Williams & Company: "Get out of line." Juleyka spent more than eighteen years in media at places such as NPR, the *Atlantic*, and Random House. But after all that time, she realized that she was stuck.

"I had spent almost my entire career as a managing something," Juleyka tells me. "My jobs had always been about the doing. Yes, I got to *execute* on ideas, but principally I was a worker bee—a high-level, middle management worker bee."

Juleyka realized she needed a way out. "I wanted an opportunity to lead with my ideas instead of a to-do list. Starting my company was the only way I was going to do that."

Once Juleyka came to that realization, she didn't immediately put in her two weeks' notice. To the contrary, she argues that getting out of line requires both internal and external preparation. Among the questions Juleyka recommends posing to yourself: "What do I have that strengthens me? What do I have that drives me? Do I have enough of a drive to grow something out of that?"

Additionally, you must assess your personal tolerance for risk, she counsels. "That is the beast, and those of us who come from immigrant backgrounds have to especially deal with it," Juleyka says. If you were raised in a home where steady employment and two weeks of paid vacation was the American dream, walking away from whatever security you have can be really hard, no matter how stuck or undervalued you feel. Juleyka, as it turned out, had an exceptionally high appetite for risk, and so she plowed ahead.

Then there is the external preparation. How will you support yourself in the period between where you are and where you're going? Juleyka stayed at her job for several months after she knew she needed to leave, and she used that time to her advantage. She showed up and kept executing on the to-do list. At the same time, she "apprenticed" herself to the job, which presented an opportunity to learn a host of new skills. She immersed herself in the audio component of the work, spending as much time as she could in studio, tethered to a more seasoned producer, so that when she left, she would bring with her those relevant skills. "Psychologically, that helped a lot," she tells me. And she used that time to make a financial plan for her business, incorporate her company, and begin feeling out potential opportunities.

Once Juleyka finally did leave, all of that plotting and planning fell into place. She emailed everyone she knew and told them the company was open for business. She continued with several editing, writing, and producing side hustles to pay herself. She also dipped into her savings and essentially "made a long-term investment in myself and my ideas, treating my company like a future high-dividend asset." She committed to growing her investment, even if it took time. Soon thereafter, she also secured a major grant from the MacArthur Foundation. Lantigua Williams & Company wasn't just open for business; it had business.

Juleyka understood her worth; she got tired of telling everyone what she could do and instead she showed them. As someone who met Juleyka only after her epiphany and subsequent liberation, it's hard to imagine that that much talent was ever parked at the back of a line. It's nearly impossible to envision that anyone thought this brilliant ideas person was best utilized as a doer. It's silly to think that her potential was ever limited by an organization's imagination because now, operating outside of that structure, it feels damn near limitless.

CHAPTER 9

Shifting Away from Likeability

Reese Witherspoon says she is "allergic" to the word "likeable"—and with good reason: it is deeply limiting. "I've sat through millions of development meetings where people are like: 'We don't want Reese to say profanity. We don't want her to have sex. We don't want her to take drugs,'" Witherspoon told writer Cara Buckley in a 2014 *New York Times* interview. "I didn't really feel the constraints of it until about three years ago, where I realized, 'I'm not this.' I'm a complex person that has so many different aspects in my personality. But somehow, I have this reductive experience where I'm put into this tiny little box."

That box, of course, was that of a likeable woman. Witherspoon had spent the early part of her career charming audiences by playing wholesome-ish, self-possessed, peppy characters like *Election*'s Tracy Flick and *Legally Blonde*'s Elle Woods. Executives didn't want to tarnish Witherspoon's "good girl" status, and so to preserve it, they put her in a boring box, one that she ultimately exploded out of by producing films that allowed her to be complicated, morally ambiguous, and at times unlikeable.

For most of us nonstarlets, these exact examples might not apply, but swap profanity, drug use, or sex on camera for "angry outbursts in a meeting" or "makes demands" and it's the same deal. Don't be complex and whole; be palatable and passable.

Witherspoon has become a sort of poster child for eschewing likeability. In 2015, she gave a speech at *Glamour*'s Woman of the Year awards in which she encouraged the audience to choose ambition, to be more ambitious, and to raise their daughters to do the same.

On one hand, I want to tell you that Reese Witherspoon found a pot of gold on the other side of the likeability rainbow: the film *Wild*, which she produced and starred in (complete with the on-air acts she'd been cautioned against), received rave reviews, grossed more than $37 million domestically, and earned Witherspoon an Academy Award nomination for Best Actress. It would be easy to use Reese as proof that we all ought to throw a concern for likeability to the wind.

On the other hand, Witherspoon's expansive career was buoyed by the perception that she was likeable. Would it all be the same if she'd started her career with *Wild* and ended it with *Legally Blonde 2*? What if the actual lesson from Witherspoon's ascension is that sometimes you have to play by the rules and meet expectations long enough to get to the point where you no longer have to play by someone else's rules?

The lesson I take away from Reese's experience isn't necessarily to forsake likeability; it's that there are things to be gained from prioritizing *other* qualities over likeability. For Reese, that was authenticity, complexity, and with it, lots and lots of money and critical acclaim.

Throughout my conversations with women leaders, I noticed that many of them are focused on intangible goals that are still much more attainable than likeability.

SELF-AWARENESS

When Mindy Grossman took over the Home Shopping Network (HSN) in 2006, most of her friends thought she had lost it. She was leaving a high-level job at Nike, a prestigious legacy brand, to, in her words, "a company many people associated with selling thighmasters." She would be the eighth CEO in ten years. The company was in disarray: sales were down, the brand had no cachet, and staff morale was low.

Mindy took swift and decisive action. She sold off distressed assets. She repositioned the brand to be more aspirational. She adjusted the product mix: Sephora was in; muumuus were out.

But as she made those moves, she also needed to engage and motivate her employees. She brought in a dumpster and had everyone throw out all the crap that accumulates when you've been in an office too long. She had the buildings power-washed and painted white. She bought every employee a new office chair. In the retelling, it all sounds like a magical fairy godmother just bippity-boppity-boo'ing about a corporate headquarters in St. Petersburg, Florida. Except changing the company's culture meant more than giving the office a face-lift; it meant firing people.

Mindy divided the company's employees into three groups:

"evangelists," employees who loved HSN, believed in the brand, and simply needed the right leadership; "wait-and-sees," employees who could go either way and were given a finite amount of time to get with the program; and "blockers," employees who were negative to the point of being toxic, and needed to be fired.

Rather than focus on how others felt about her decision, she focused on making sure others understood her vision for the future of the company and how they could support that vision. "Am I painting a clear enough vision?" she asked herself. "Am I articulating why each person needs to be part of that vision? Am I giving people tools to do the job they need to do?"

As Mindy worked to right the ship, and as the company went public in 2008, another wave hit: the financial crisis. "There were six thousand people, their families and their communities, depending on us to move the company forward, regardless of the environment. I felt that on my shoulders," Mindy tells me. "How I showed up, and how I comported myself and how I communicated, and the confidence that I showed was critical. Those are the times where you have to sublimate some of what you're really feeling because anyone in that time frame was concerned. There was a lot chaos. Was the world going to come out of this? Those are the times that you actually have to be the strongest in articulating. You can't say everything is going to be great. You have to say: 'Here's the vision. Here's what I need you to do. Here are the tough decisions that we have to make.' There's a need for a combination of stoic leadership and a certain level of transparency and empathy."

Even with those additional stressors, she managed to turn the company around. She took what was a home shopping channel and reimagined it as a digital company. Under her leadership, HSN stopped losing millions of dollars a year. By

2016, the company was earning more than $100 million. The accolades followed: *Financial Times* named Mindy one of the top fifty women in world business. She's been on *Forbes*'s list of most powerful women in the world several times over.

As we sit in her New York City offices at Weight Watchers, where Mindy is now the CEO, I am trying to figure out how the same person who buys an employee a Herman Miller Aeron chair to boost morale can also identify other employees as "toxic" and push them out the door without blinking. How one person can be stoic and empathetic, strong and warm, in a moment of crisis.

As I probe, Mindy offers me a variety of philosophies: She advocates "a culture of generosity. Focus on making other people successful, and you inherently become more successful," she tells me. "Never let anyone walk out of the room feeling diminished," she warns. I am buying everything she, a persuasive speaker and a natural saleswoman, is selling. Perhaps it is the majesty of her head-to-toe jewel tones, or her perfect blowout, or the fact that she is casually texting with Oprah, a Weight Watchers shareholder, but I cannot help but feel that I am getting one-on-one coaching from someone who is as much a spiritual guru as a business leader.

In this grab bag of hard-earned wisdom, there is one declaration that feels most relevant to the question of what makes Mindy so appealing. "Your greatest power," Mindy tells me, "is your self-awareness of who you are and your impact on people." That makes sense in the context of what she has told me: she sees herself as a disruptor, but also a kind and generous person. She judges her legacy at HSN not by the people she had to disappoint, but by the people whose jobs she saved as the economy went into free fall. It's all about perspective.

Mindy admits that she was not always as self-aware as she is today. One of the hardest transitions was her jump from Ralph Lauren's Polo jeans to Nike. "I went from being the CEO of a $450 million division, to this giant global, matrixed male-dominated company. It was a little tricky to maneuver," she says. So Mindy, an advocate of "perpetual self-improvement," asked the head of HR to hire her an executive coach.

She received a 360-degree evaluation, a process that includes input from subordinates, colleagues, supervisors, and the employees. It's like inviting everyone to say what they say about you behind your back to your face.

Upon receiving the results of her evaluation, Mindy focused on the negative elements, and played the inevitable game of who gave which pieces of feedback. But as she processed the results, it became less about her, and more about her effect on others. "What it was telling me was what my impact was and what I could do better." Among the things Mindy learned about herself: She would ask employees for feedback, but not give them sufficient time to articulate their views. She would quickly jump to "here's what we need to do," not giving others time to weigh in, and once she, the boss, had spoken, it felt futile. She was assigning tasks without fully appreciating the limits of the organization's capacity.

So she modified her behavior accordingly. Mostly she taught herself to slow down, but she also learned how to manage others around her preferences and needs, asking for materials in advance, helping expedite meetings before they started.

"It's nice to be liked," Mindy tells me, sensing that I am still grasping for the answer of how she gets to be her, hoping she can give me an Oprah-style nugget of wisdom. "But not everybody is going to like everybody else. If you're real, if your intent is true, if you're doing things for the right reason and people respect and value you, that to me is really important."

CLARITY

If there was one consistent belief among the women leaders I spoke with, it is that a hyperemphasis on likeability is detrimental not only to one's success, but to one's efficacy as a leader. They came to those conclusions both through their own experience and by watching other women whose workplace choices prioritized keeping others happy over the actual outcome.

As president and CEO of the Robert Wood Johnson Foundation, the largest health-focused philanthropy in the United States, Dr. Risa Lavizzo-Mourey became well versed in the art of difficult decisions. In her nearly fifteen years at the organization, she made personnel changes. She navigated the politics of a bipartisan foundation, sometimes catching heat on the left, and sometimes heat from the right. She often had to tell grantees, contractors, and staff "no." "It was usually in the context of those decisions that I would hear 'she's difficult,'" Lavizzo-Mourey tells me. But she insists that's part of the job. "When people don't get the exact outcome that they want, they can see that as a difficult situation. If you're never described as difficult for being willing to take a stand, it's hard to be a respected leader."

"Criticism is part of the price of leadership," Carly Fiorina tells me. "The higher you go in an organization, the more visible you become, the more risks you need to take to achieve the results, the more opportunity there is to criticize. When you are in a position of senior leadership, your job actually is not to be liked by everyone. Your job is to lead. And so you end up having to make decisions that not everyone agrees with, not everyone likes, and in some cases people are negatively impacted by. It's hard to like someone who's laying you off. It's hard to like someone in the moment who's telling you that you don't get a promotion, you don't get a raise." And yet, she'd argue, those decisions are necessary.

In my personal experience and in my conversation with others, I recognize how often two very different goals become easily conflated. Many people who care about likeability also care deeply about how their words and their actions impact others. That awareness of others is worth applauding. Our world could use more of it.

Where that care for others' feelings gets perverted is when that awareness actually limits an individual from being truthful. Concern for how you make others feel and creating a desired image of yourself in someone else's mind are not one and the same. Yes, your ideal may be to support others and in turn hope that they see you as the kind and likeable person you are. But sometimes it is impossible to achieve both goals.

A "compassionate goal" improves the well-being of another. That's different than being nice, which is about how others perceive you and how you perceive yourself. Sometimes a compassionate goal requires addressing hard truths: seeking treatment for a loved one struggling with addiction, or telling HR that a coworker is creating a toxic work environment. Sometimes doing the right thing and being nice are in direct opposition. Sometimes the things we need to do to do right by others, to be truly compassionate, mean that we won't be liked.

Making decisions predicated exclusively on minimizing conflict only kicks conflict down the road. There are situations where great leadership requires the type of truth-telling and bold action that will invariably hurt someone's feelings and put someone out. Just because people don't like the decision, it doesn't mean that they don't like you or that they won't respect you for making the tough calls.

And for those whose work is about social causes, rather than a bottom line, very often the work itself requires disagreement and conflict.

What these leaders had was clarity: they were clear on their objective, they were clear on the tough choices that needed to be made to get there, and they were clear in their belief that the intended outcome of their action was ultimately in the best interest of the institution and the people they lead. Worrying too much about what others think can muddy the process of making a hard decision. Strip that element away, focus on your goal, clarify your intent, and suddenly the road clears.

RELATABILITY AND THE POWER OF CONNECTION

In 2012 I interviewed Mindy Kaling, the actress, writer, and producer who came to prominence on *The Office*, and later on her own show, *The Mindy Project*, onstage at Lincoln Center in New York as part of the Women in the World summit. During our interview, I asked why we don't see more women characters on television who may be flawed and messy on the margins but who fundamentally have their act together.

Mindy responded, "I'm in an industry where likeability is the most paramount thing you can have in a lead." There was that word. I didn't even have to bring it up. "And often likeability," Mindy continued, "is when people feel like you're an underdog and . . . your life is a mess." Then she pivoted back to the real world. "I also think that if you take the average person who creates a show—it is such a Herculean task to put a show on the air, have it stay on the air—and that type of personality is not a mess. There's this feeling when you're doing it of like, okay, no one wants to see a type-A decisive creative person on TV because it's not soft and likeable."

It was like she was seeing my type-A soul.

"You brought up the concept of likeability," I said, as though

Mindy hadn't been present for the answer she'd given a moment before, "and it's something that I think a lot about. I too want desperately for people to like me." Now three thousand of my new closest friends knew this truth. "When you're on television, you have numbers that show you whether or not people like you, which can, you know, make you go crazy." Mindy nodded along as though we shared a therapist, "Great. Great. Really good for your psychology."

"And so I wonder, off air, I mean, do you care?" I asked, now totally off script. "Especially in this age of endless feedback on social media, and ratings. Do you care about being likeable?" I expected her to say yes. What she said was more interesting.

"I don't care about being likeable so much as I care about being relatable," Mindy replied without hesitation. "I think that they're often confused, but they're very different ideas. To me, relatable means that even if you do something that some people might say is unconscionable, if you're sitting in the audience, you're like, 'You know what? I have done that.'"

Convincing executives to see it that way is a different challenge. "You'll get notes from the network—they just want you to be sweet," Mindy said. "But that's because they're not creative. You have to find ways of saying, you know, my character can do insane stuff. One of the great gifts of comedy is that if it's posed in the right way, if it comes from something you've actually done, the leap you make is that someone has done it, too."

I had never thought about relatability as it relates to likeability. And yet so much of my own desire to be liked comes from a desire to be understood, to be relatable.

Once asked about the divisive nature of two of her protagonists' romantic affair, Shonda Rhimes replied, "I don't worry about whether or not it makes them likeable. Traditional network television tries to make our main characters likeable because people are afraid if you're not likeable, I don't know, no one's going to watch them. I just think it makes people interesting."

If you knew you had to choose between being interesting and being universally likeable, which would you choose? Which would you prioritize in an employee? Are you hoping to hire a bunch of bots who are all pleasant or a team of humans who are complex and nuanced, and bring that complexity and nuance to their work?

KNOW WHOSE OPINION MATTERS

Part of having clarity is knowing, for yourself, whose opinion matters. At work, that can take many forms. For some, it is a strategic interoffice decision: Who do I need to maintain a positive relationship with in order to get my work done? To advance? For others, it is about a broader landscape: balancing the needs of clients, employees, managers, board members, or investors. For political organizers, especially those who fight for the most marginalized communities, the work requires clarity about who they serve and advocate for.

Regardless of how this manifests in your world, there is value in clarifying how you are weighting the feedback and competing signals you receive.

In Sabrina Hersi Issa's work in politics, philanthropy, and as a partner at a venture capital firm, she's seen firsthand how much it matters to have others acting as advocates for you. People who get their ideas invested in and their projects sponsored have what Sabrina calls "table bangers." They have individuals at the table, thumping the table for them, ready to cheer on their ideas. "That's what I have found informative," Sabrina tells me. "Even if my excellence is undisputed, I need people at the table, banging for me." Understanding this, Sabrina would rather collect a small number of champions than try to be liked by everyone.

YOU MATTER

Lest you need to be reminded: *you* are a person who matters.

Rebecca Cokley, who now works as the director of the Disability Justice Initiative at the Center for American Progress, is often asked to speak at public events. At a disability policy event on Capitol Hill, event organizers, who knew of Cokley's disability, provided her with a standard-sized podium from which to offer her remarks. Her options were to stand next to the podium, trying to balance her notes in one hand and the microphone in the other, or to stand behind the podium where no one would be able to see her. Both options were terrible. Cokley decided to make a point of illustrating the organizers' oversight and stood behind the podium. "I don't care," she says with a laugh. "You can show this on C-SPAN."

Now, when Cokley is slated to speak at events, she requests a table, a microphone, and a ramp to the stage. "When I was young I never would have been this way," Cokley says of asking for what she needs. "I would have felt that I was asking for special treatment or that I was putting people out by asking. But I saw the men in my community ask for things. I thought, 'Wait, I can do that? I can ask for that?' There's power in that. I'm setting an example for the women with a disability coming up behind me."

Sabrina has a not dissimilar story. She was invited to speak at a conference in Austria, and when she arrived, she learned that the conference organizers had booked her at a hotel forty-five minutes away. Sabrina wheeled her suitcase into the conference center and asked to be moved to a hotel closer to the conference. When the organizers resisted, Sabrina asked why a white male peer she had traveled with was offered accommodations nearby. "That is very easy to explain," the organizer told her. "He is more important than you." (Mind you, this person was a fellow political operative, not a world leader.) The organizers claimed that every nearby hotel and inn was sold out. Sabrina made a decision: if they could not find her suitable accommodations, she would not speak at the conference. She would pay the change fee on her airplane ticket and return home the next day.

After what Sabrina calls a "multi-hour entrenchment," during which she explained that she was a black woman traveling solo in a foreign country in which she did not speak the language and did not feel safe being so far from civilization, the organizers finally put her in a nearby hotel. I tell Sabrina that I hope I would advocate for myself as she advocated for herself, but I admit that even once the situation was resolved, I'd likely worry about the fallout. Sabrina understands this. Afterward, she tells me, she did think that she would never be invited back and that she'd be known as a difficult person. "All of that is okay with me," Sabrina tells me. "That is a cost that I will pay to be safe. My needs are met. If this is the path that I had to take to get those needs met, that says something more about them."

Sabrina understood her own worth, she valued her own safety, and that made asking for what she needed even easier.

NO NEW FALSE CHOICES

Much of this book is premised on invalidating false choices. By presenting self-awareness, relatability, and clarity as alternatives to likeability, I don't mean to suggest that you actually have to choose between them. I also don't mean that you have to pursue all of them all at once. The last thing you need is that kind of to-do.

Instead, we have to start asking what being told to prioritize likeability is costing women, and what we all might gain by that shift in perspective. Do you want a woman with incredible potential to spend her waking hours thinking about the way her voice sounds? Or, presuming she is not a singer or a voice-over artist, do you want her to work on the skills that actually impact her results?

While we women are working on our style, many of our colleagues are instead working on their hard skills. What would happen if managers redirected all of the time and energy spent mentoring women and instead focused on sponsoring them by putting them on the best projects and the best teams and advocating for their promotions? What if women were allowed to lead, exactly as they are? How high could we fly if no one was clipping our wings?

CHAPTER 10

What We Can Do, as Individuals and as Organizations

Given how much "lady in the workplace" advice focuses on what women can do to fix themselves and improve their circumstances, I will not pretend that women can solve this problem on their own, nor should they be required to. But there are steps that we can take as individuals, especially those of us who have a modicum of access to power, to begin to collectively address these challenges. We can make sure we aren't perpetuating the problem, we can step in when we identify bias disguised as a question of likeability, and we can encourage organizations to look at how they offer feedback and assess employees. Most of the work needs to be done at the organizational level, but it will take individuals demanding that change to make it happen.

WHAT YOU CAN DO FOR OTHERS

Natalia Oberti Noguera is the founder and CEO of Pipeline Angels, a company that is working to change the face of angel investing. Her commitment to diversity and pushing boundaries is baked into everything she does. In a taping for *Latina to Latina*, I asked how she became comfortable with making people uncomfortable. Natalia is a self-identified cis queer Latina. "I, being me, gives people discomfort," she told me. Sitting at the intersection of multiple marginalized identities, Natalia regularly contends with structural racism and homophobia. Her response is to confront those biases in order to make room for others.

When I described likeability as a luxury to Natalia, she challenged me to also think of it as a privilege. Anyone who is part of a dominant culture or, like me, has the ability to shape-shift, to make themselves palatable to the powers that be, must at some point use that privilege on behalf of those for whom fitting in is not an option. I must think to myself—if I have been granted access to power, what do I plan to do with it? If I generally make people comfortable, I have the capacity to challenge their assumptions and biases about those who don't have the same luxury. What do I want to do with that power?

CHECK YOURSELF AND CALL IT OUT

None of us are immune to unconscious bias. Before we can be helpful in addressing others' bias or institutional bias, we have to take stock of our own. Who do we prefer working with? Why? How much do we allow those preferences to guide our choices around hiring, assignments, and promotions? As managers, do we give everyone a true chance to weigh in?

And when it comes specifically to language: are the words we use to describe workers different based on their gender? If so, Catalyst offers a variety of helpful tips for shifting the way we talk about women at work. For example, if you find a conversation about a woman colleague is focused on her style (so aggressive!), redirect the conversation to focus instead on her work performance (she has really motivated the team to up their game). Rather than praise a woman by calling her "helpful," which limits her to a support role, choose to highlight her actual contributions (she did all the research that the report was based on).

And the same advice that Caterina Kostoula suggests you yourself use to receive critical subjective feedback can apply to what you observe is said about other women. When a colleague describes a woman's style, ask them to be more concrete. Ask what the impact is on her work. Or use my favorite inquiry: "Compared to whom?"

Look around at meetings. Which perspectives are missing? Who should be in the room but isn't? Invite those people in, or suggest to the meeting organizer that they be included. The same goes for networking events, conferences, and panels. The Time's Up Plus One Initiative encourages professional women to invite another woman to events that will give her access and exposure and expand her network. Let her show her appreciation by dousing you both with hand sanitizer after. If you're invited to speak on a panel, ask which other perspectives will be included. Who is missing? A conversation on the power of the Latinx market with no Afro-Latinas? A discussion of media representation with no queer women? Point it out to the organizers. Suggest individuals who can bring that perspective, and encourage them to include her, even if it requires giving up your spot.

BE A SPONSOR OR "TABLE BANG" FOR OTHER WOMEN

As we move up the ranks, it can be easy to forget that we are now the ones in charge. We may not be in the C-suite just yet, but we have political capital. I want to dare you to use it, especially for those who show promise and need it most.

For those of us in organizational systems, that means not just admiring another woman's contributions to the team, but admiring them out loud, to others in a way that connects the dots between her excellence and her advancement. Put her forward for big assignments. Recommend her for promotions. Make sure others inside the organization know about her accomplishments. Give her air cover when she is about to take a big risk.

For those of us who operate outside of a more traditional office hierarchy (I'm looking at you, creatives, freelancers, politicos), do the same for a woman in your industry. Recommend her for projects. Introduce her to people she needs to know, those who won't just give her more feedback, but people who are willing to open doors, provide her with funding, or hire her.

And if sponsorship feels too formal, too cumbersome, or too transactional, find a way to express the underlying principle. To borrow a phrase from Sabrina Hersi Issa: "Table-bang." Be so enthusiastic about a woman and her ideas that it becomes impossible to ignore them. Bang all the physical and metaphorical tables for her. Say her name so many times in so many rooms that you begin to forget it is her name and not yours.

WHAT ORGANIZATIONS CAN DO

Reimagining leadership and advocating for diversity in the workplace cannot fall only on the shoulders of women and minorities. Research shows that while executives in general do not benefit from advocating for diversity, when nonwhites and women advocate for others like them to join their ranks they are actually penalized. In a follow-up study, participants were asked to rate a fictitious manager on their hiring decisions. The managers who were women and/or who were not white were perceived as less competent when they hired a minority candidate. The white male managers? There was no penalty regardless of who they hired. As the authors of the study put it, "Basically, all managers were judged harshly if they hired someone who looked like them, unless they were a white male."

Tracy Chou, as she has developed a public platform focused on diversity and inclusion, has paid a price as an engineer. "It was hard for me to gain credibility internally for engineering work if people also knew about my public presence on other topics. Even if I was doing my job and delivering on all milestones, people would assume that I wasn't really committed," Tracy told me. "I felt like I needed to overperform in my engineering work to earn the right to even talk about diversity."

The responsibility for creating a legitimately inclusive workplace begins with those at the very top truly embracing inclusion as a priority, one that is good for business. Google spent two years analyzing team performance and found that the highest-performing teams had one thing in common: psychological safety. The teams that did best were those where people felt encouraged and supported to be honest and open and to take risks. "When you have an environment that has high psychological safety, you can genuinely harness diverse perspectives," Daisy Auger-Dominguez, who led diversity staffing and inclusion strategies at Google, tells me. "There's an expanded body of research and popular discussion about the benefits of workforce diversity. Namely that more diversity leads to more diverse perspectives, which lead to increased creativity and innovation. Well, that only happens when people can be themselves."

Daisy argues that much of that culture shift happens not just in systems or in processes, but in a fundamental understanding of and agreement around what is institutionally important and acceptable. What is considered "normal" behavior? Does an organization recognize, take responsibility for, and then accept or reject toxic behavior? Is there objectivity in decision-making processes? Is there transparency around how decisions are made? How do you make sure that everyone feels like their perspective matters?

Researchers found that psychological safety relied on two group practices: emotional connection and taking equal turns in conversation. "I've seen the light shine in someone when they feel included," Auger-Dominguez says. "You want my opinion? You're asking me to engage? Folks are not used to that. The goal is to do that in a way that is more systematic and consistent."

There is a lot of literature dedicated to the question of tackling unconscious bias and creating an inclusive workspace. These are some of the solutions that resonate most with me.

BAKE SPONSORSHIP INTO YOUR ORGANIZATIONAL CULTURE

Sponsorship is critical for women and minorities, and yet particularly hard to win or cultivate when there aren't a lot of people in the senior ranks who look like you or share your life experience. People of color report being more ambitious than their white peers, but undersponsored. For example, only 11 percent of black women report having sponsors, a number that is striking when you consider how ambitious black women have to be, given how much trouble they have simply being seen inside of majority-white spaces. Without a sponsor, will anyone even see their work?

Although African-Americans, Latinx, and Asians in senior leadership feel more responsibility to sponsor than their white peers, they are less likely to actually do it. Sadly, this is in part because these leaders doubt whether they have the capital necessary to help propel others. There is also trepidation on the part of minorities seeking sponsors over having a minority sponsor—will their assent be seen as a product of "favoritism" based on shared background rather than ability?

That's why it must be incumbent upon organizations to set standards for sponsorship, ones that encourage employees to invest in sponsorship and to overcome their own internalized bias about who is worthy of such investment.

ADDRESS SUBJECTIVITY IN PERFORMANCE REVIEWS AND FOCUS ON RESULTS

Much of the bias expressed as questions of likeability happens in interactions and exchanges that are so mundane it might be easy to miss them altogether. But one of the easier places to formally identify this bias is in formal processes, like performance reviews.

"My worst moments have been when I am trying to be what I think someone wants me to be," Amanda, the tech executive who has been overwhelmed by stylistic feedback, says. Most recently, she was told that she needed to more aggressively manage underperformers. From Amanda's perspective, she *was* managing them, but she was doing it one-on-one, creating space for team members to implement her feedback. That logic didn't appease her manager, who insisted that Amanda BCC him on all emails to her team. "I need to *see* you being more aggressive," Amanda's manager told her.

Amanda complied. She gave her team very direct feedback in order to prove to her boss that she was being appropriately aggressive. Only it didn't feel right to Amanda. "I still feel sick to my stomach when I think about it," Amanda says.

Here's the thing: Amanda was getting results. "If he needed me to get there faster that would have been fair game for feedback," Amanda says. "But saying 'You're getting there, but I need you to do it more aggressively,' To what end? So that I can be some inauthentic person and put everybody else through hell while I'm at it?" This experience made Amanda want to focus instead on managing her team around results.

Among the most common refrains I heard throughout my interviews was a plea from women to have their performance evaluated on the results they deliver rather than on the way they manage and lead. Workers benefit from formalized feedback, but we know that performance reviews are subjective and riddled with bias. So how do you keep the constructive and critical objective feedback that reviews can offer and shake the bias?

Clear Objectives

Ensure that the criteria for a review are well articulated and objective. Make sure evaluators are trained and have the tools to describe which behaviors and results are being evaluated, and how. Tie the criteria to outcomes. "You have a tendency to shy away from conflict" is not nearly as helpful as "When you shied away from resolving the dispute between Molly and Hal, the team fractured, leading to a delay in getting the deck to the client."

Frequent Feedback

Very often feedback is given once a year or, even worse, exclusively when things go wrong. What if, instead, you received feedback on a regular basis?

"If you set up a system where critical feedback is an integral part of your culture at an organization and you make it something that happens often and consistently, it becomes less of a tool to punish people and more of a development tool," Lily Jampol tells me. "It allows people to be a little bit less threatened on both sides."

With frequent reviews there are more data points for a manager to assess: Was the employee's performance consistent over the course of the year? Did she improve? Was she able to put feedback into practice? And for the employee, there is the possibility of identifying and correcting behavior in real time. If you're doing something wrong, do you want to keep doing it over and over again from January to December? Or do you want to be given an opportunity to improve throughout the year?

Crowdsource

Rather than having a solo manager conduct a review, multiple members of a team (in some cases, even a client) who all know the employee's work firsthand should be able to offer insights about an individual's performance. Think of it this way: if an employee has only one person, presumably their manager, weigh in on their work, they're only getting their take. If that employee and manager are two peas in a pod, then the employee is more likely to get a positive review. (However, even that feedback, while affirming, might be useless if it is based on shared personal preference rather than a critical assessment of skills and results.) If an employee and their manager have different styles, then an employee may be out of luck. By developing a wider circle of those who assess an individual's performance, they are more likely to get feedback from those who share their style *and* those who don't, creating a more complex and complete picture of their work.

While it's useful to know how an employee interacts with the person who manages them, it's also helpful for everyone to have a sense of how that employee interacts with those lateral to them, those they manage, and those with whom they work less frequently. An individual may be very strong in one direction and struggle in another. Plus, different employees bring different expertise and, with that, different lenses of analysis.

Let me back it way up for a minute: most places I have worked did not have formal performance reviews. Most of my insights into my own strengths and weaknesses have come from on-the-fly feedback that was often circumstantial and rarely wholistic. Political campaigns aren't intended to be multiyear projects. You're just sprinting to November. I've never known anyone to do reviews, even as part of a postmortem. At that point you're either packing up your apartment and looking for your next job or drowning your sorrows in stale donuts. Often both. When I left the nonprofit world, some management consultant best practices had begun to creep in, but in general, there weren't formal reviews. In television newsrooms, taking time to think about an employee's big-picture contributions can feel esoteric when you are constantly measuring people by their contributions on a show-to-show basis. Unfortunately, in the absence of formalized reviews the likes of which I now understand to be normal in other professional spaces, employees are often left to guess about whether or not their contributions are sufficient or exceptional.

In addition, not all industries and workplaces have "results" and "metrics" that can be tabulated and assessed. Producing, for example, can arguably be judged by ratings, virality, or pickup by other outlets, but sometimes someone has done a great job and none of those things happen. Some of the way we evaluate content is inevitably subjective based on our interests and our priorities. "In a competitive business, performance actually counts. Results count," Carly Fiorina told me. "So if you can produce results, solve problems, deliver performance, people over time—I have learned—will dismiss the style." But Fiorina concedes that there are also organizations where tangible results are difficult to demonstrate. "In that situation it frequently does become all about who follows the process, who plays the game, who sucks up the best. Those environments are very, very difficult."

Not every workplace utilizes performance reviews, nor does every line of work render demonstrable results. But the necessary shift in how managers think about their employees is the same. In situations where the feedback is less formalized, managers need to make an even greater effort to assess employees based on performance. They need to acknowledge and challenge their own biases about "the right way" to manage and to lead. That is made less amorphous by following the basic guidelines above: give frequent feedback, tie feedback to outcomes, and try to allow others who have a different vantage point on the work and the workers to contribute to your understanding of the role an individual plays.

By recognizing bias and the limits of free-form feedback, and actively working to make reviews less subjective, managers are empowered to give better feedback and employees are better equipped to improve their approach to work.

I'd argue that there is an additional benefit, too. By shifting to objective metrics and by tying feedback to outcomes, employers and managers open up the possibility of seeing a person's natural leadership style as a thing of value. If an aggressive woman gets results, well then, aren't you glad she's aggressive? There's research that suggests that women attorneys

who act with agency don't contend with the likeability penalty.
(Note: when I mentioned this to female attorneys they were
skeptical.) A client wants their representative to go to the mat
for them—to make their case, to outmaneuver their adversary,
to secure them the best deal. When aggression and directness
are in the service of a third party, people kinda dig this quality
in women. And for women who are naturally more communal,
if that spirit is facilitating team building and yielding results,
why ask her to change?

All of these seemingly small changes—a larger individual and
cultural awareness of how likeability can be a cover for bias,
self-assessing where our own biases get crossed with likeability, calling out others' bias, finding and being a sponsor, and
examining the mechanisms of formalized feedback—can add
up to big change. It is the most tangible change we can pursue in our day-to-day work lives while the even bigger seismic
shifts are under way.

CHAPTER 11

Let Her Lead

Do me a favor. Take out a piece of paper. On it, draw an effective leader. Yes, that's the only prompt I'm giving you. Go! Doodle it in the margins if you must. I'll wait.

Waiting.

Waiting.

Doing calisthenics to pass the time.

Okay, let's see your masterpiece.

This exercise, originally stumbled upon by Tina Kiefer, a professor of organizational behavior, almost always yields the same results: asked to draw an effective leader, most people draw a man. Even when participants draw images that are gender neutral, the language referring to the image tends to be masculine. When they imagined a leader, they imagined men.

Many if not most women who strive to lead have felt this bias in action. They know that they have to prove themselves as leaders to be seen as leaders. And yet, many of the things that women do in order to prove their substance and value inadvertently undermines others' views of them. A woman focuses on the details to prove her competence, or she acts collaboratively to avoid the success penalty, and her reward is that she is not seen as a visionary. For all of the hand-wringing and feedback around our appearance, our voice, our posture, and the style we employ to manage our teams, there is still this truth: even when women act the part, and even when they go to great lengths to compensate for perceived limitations, there is no guarantee that others will see them as a person who ought to be in charge.

When most people imagine leaders, they imagine white, straight men. What would it take to change that?

This is the true challenge at the heart of the likeability and success paradox: so long as "leadership" is considered synonymous with supposedly masculine qualities, it will be incredibly challenging for women to be seen as leaders, especially in male-dominated fields. Women will either act the way society expects women to act and be told they're not leaderly enough, or they'll act the way society expects men to act and they'll be penalized for violating gender expectations. If they try to change, they risk sacrificing their authenticity. If they refuse to change, they risk being deemed intractable.

A woman can choose:

Be herself or be well liked; be herself or be perceived as a leader; express her anger or be well liked; express her anger or be perceived as a leader; be authentic or be well liked; be authentic or be perceived as a leader; ask for what she wants or be well liked; ask for what she needs or be well liked; be ambitious or be well liked; be successful or be well liked.

Every single one of those supposed choices is lose-lose. So how do we make it win-win?

The answer isn't straightforward, and it isn't immediate.

Too often we tell women how they can alter their presentation styles to increase their chances of having their potential acknowledged. It's why there's so much advice about how to approach pivotal career points, such as interviews, promotions, and negotiations, in a way that gets a woman what she deserves without turning others off. This well-intended counsel can be helpful for those of us who are living these challenges right now. But I worry that it's distracting us from the more fundamental shift.

For this same reason—the slow-going change of reimagining leadership—it feels so liberating to just encourage women to care less about what others think of them. Stop caring and do your own thing. Boom! Problem solved. It feels as though it allows us to reclaim power almost instantly.

But as we've discussed, there's virtually no defined process for learning to care less. The work of learning to care less about how others perceive you is deep and, dare I say, spiritual. It's not just a thing you decide and then do. It requires years of undoing and unlearning. Even more important, this prescription ignores the penalties that remain in hiring, in assignments, in assessments, in promotions for women who are dubbed unlikeable or not leaderly or who simply refuse to change. A woman can alter her approach to likeability, but she is still subject to penalty if the world around her does not change as well.

If we want different types of people to be able to lead—women, nonbinary people, mothers, sensitive men, men of color—then we need to reconsider what this emphasis on likeability and its narrow definition is costing us. We need a more dynamic shift to create space for those who do not conform to society's expectations of who a leader is. To close the trapdoors of likeability requires a radical reimagining of leadership, one that disentangles leadership from traditional white masculinity.

We need to think of "strength" as a quality that takes more than one shape, one that can be as quiet as it is blustery. We need to see someone who has all of the qualities of a Laura—intuition, warmth, tenacity—and think, "Wow, that is compelling." We must reimagine leadership to include leaders who are gentle, empathetic, and kind. In doing that, we have to expand our notions of some very ingrained concepts. We need to recognize that "toughness" is as much about grit as it is about sternness.

It strikes me that when I asked Valerie Jarrett about her friend and colleague Cecilia Muñoz, the two words Jarrett used to describe Muñoz were "humane" and "tough." Not the yeller, not the screamer, not the desk pounder, but still, tough as nails.

In that definitional expansion, we need to allow women who are, by nature, assertive and direct to use those qualities to their organization's benefit without fear of social alienation. We need to encourage the Michelles to ask, to challenge, and to confront without worrying that the same thing that makes them good at their jobs makes them outcasts in their own offices. We need to give workers permission to express anger and passion about the things they care about most without worrying that they'll be labeled a problem. We need to see a woman express anger in the workplace and consider among the possible explanations for it that she cares deeply and has been tipped off by an outside force. Women workers need to be allowed to have a bad day without being written off as unhinged.

Leaders can continue to squeeze themselves into boxes that do not fit, or we can blow up the boxes and create something bigger and better.

Feminist writer Jessica Valenti describes the specific conflict for women who seek to be both successful and likeable as a challenge without an easy solution. "Women's likeability is something feminists use as proof of inequity—he's a boss, she's a bitch—but not something we've put on par with standard feminist fare like reproductive rights or pay inequality," Valenti writes. "Because there's no policy you can create to make people like successful women."

She's right, and her assertion applies to the likeability challenges beyond the success penalty. There is no single policy, no quantifiable answer that addresses the traps I've identified and the many more that I have no doubt are underfoot. Of the women I interviewed, nearly all of them mused, "I'm not sure what the answer is."

I know what the answer is not: encouraging women to care more, care less, or any other prescription that shifts the full weight of fixing this problem back to the individual. In fact, recent research shows that many of the empowerment messages intended to help women succeed at work give people the impression that women are responsible for both creating the problem *and* fixing it.

LIKE A GIRL

Let's shine a light on how likeability is subjective, but it is also deeply human, and central to many of the decisions that are made throughout an individual's life, including one's career. People may always like who they like, but we can change the way that affects our sense of who deserves to lead.

The communal qualities that women are believed to bring to leadership roles are increasingly valued. And yet . . . choosing to lead in a way that values relationship and connection is still presented as a lesser and novel form of leadership.

Mike Krzyzewski, head coach of the Duke basketball team, has won five national championships and boasts more than a thousand career wins, the most in NCAA history. As head coach of the USA Men's Olympic National Team, he's won four gold medals. With this track record, he's become known as much as a leader as an athletic figure. What stands out to me about much of the analysis of Krzyzewski, or Coach K, is that others attribute much of his success to coaching and managing "like a girl." He places an emphasis on building relationships with each player, supporting emotional needs and encouraging communication.

It strikes me that doing something "like a girl" in a presumed masculine space is considered novel. Surprisingly positive! It's as though the headline writers acknowledge that to ordinarily do something "like a girl" is a dig—you run like a girl, you throw like a girl—but in this case (curveball!) it's a compliment.

What would happen if this type of leadership were considered the gold standard?

A NEW VALUE FOR "SOFT SKILLS"

If we cannot reimagine leadership, perhaps the economy will reimagine it for us. Automation, artificial intelligence (AI), and robotics are nipping at our heels, showing competence in skills ranging from sales to lawyering. J. P. Morgan now has software that can complete in a matter of seconds what it takes attorneys 360,000 hours to do. So much for that yacht you were gonna name "Billable Hours"!

Advocates of AI promise that with increased productivity comes economic growth. Humans, they argue, will be freed up from mundanity and more able to focus on big, exciting ideas.

Yet many of us can't help but worry that Little Wonder is a greater threat to our job security than that ambitious (human) intern down the hall.

Understanding the uncertainty that comes in a moment of such extreme change, Pew Research asked experts to weigh in on what America will need to do to adapt to a future where humans work alongside artificial intelligence. According to the report, "workers of the future will learn to deeply culti- vate and exploit creativity, collaborative activity, abstract and systems thinking, complex communication, and the ability to thrive in diverse environments." Put another way: in a future where work is dominated by AI, some of the biggest strategic advantages humans have will rely on their ability to connect with one another, to be uniquely human. To manage and lead the way that is most often ascribed to women.

"Given that the workplace is going through these profound changes, the wind is at our backs to create a new paradigm," Arianna Huffington tells me. "We are also in a time in which no company, no matter how established, is safe from disrup- tion. This puts a premium on building purpose and culture within companies. That's often been shunted off to the world of HR, the department most associated with women's leader- ship. But guess what? That's where the future is."

ALLOW HER TO BECOME A LEADER

Likeability in the workplace is often framed as a matter of utility. Evangelists for likeability tout its many positive uses: winning new clients, building connections that lead to part- nerships and favors, and ability to influence. But there is also something more amorphous that likeability connotes: a sense of acceptance, the feeling that we belong as we are, wherever we are. With that comfort, we feel empowered to thrive, to be our best selves, because when we are liked for being our authentic selves we feel seen; we feel known.

In the discourse around women and leadership, much of the discussion focuses on giving women the opportunity to lead. That is, of course, a critical step in the process of leapfrogging from reimagining leadership to building a world in which that leadership has been reimagined. But that framework can obscure another critical element to becoming a leader: seeing yourself as one. An individual doesn't take on the identity of a leader because they are granted a title; they take it on through a process of success and failures, of things that can seem small: accomplishing a challenging assignment, calling a meeting, or resolving a conflict. The process of becoming a leader requires being given lots of minor opportunities to step into leadership.

When given the opportunity to lead, women often prove themselves to be exceptional leaders. Plus, women in top leadership roles sometimes get an additional boost. Because executive leadership roles are seen as highly masculine and requiring tremendous competence, when a woman attains one of those roles, others often think, "Wow, she must have been *really* good to get there."

YOU WILL SURVIVE

On the brink of finishing this book, I had breakfast with one of my best friends. As we sat down, she teased me, saying, "You never interviewed me."

It turns out, I was catching her at a bad moment, or a perfect moment, depending on which one of us you were asking. After several years of positive reviews, she was for the first time told by a manager that some of her team members find her "difficult to work with." She started to tear up. We've been friends for nearly twenty years and I can count the number of times I've seen her cry on one hand. So I started to cry. She was working her ass off. Her workload was twice what it ordinarily was. She was being called difficult because the work was difficult. She was so frustrated. She was already implementing the feedback. But still, the question hung over us: *Why did this seem so hard?*

I questioned whether she should signal to someone that her workload had become too much. That was the underlying problem, right? Asking her to be more pleasant was really a cosmetic fix.

"Oh no," she told me. She had recently gone to a leadership workshop where she was coached to never admit that she is overwhelmed. "You don't say you're underwater," she told me. "You say, I've got a lot of projects going on, and they're all really interesting!"

We laughed.

And laughed.

And laughed.

I laughed so hard at the image of a woman drowning in her work and being told to smile that I cried again.

Searching for a lifesaver, I tossed my friend the only one I had.

This isn't about you, I told her.

You are not alone, I assured her.

You don't need to change, I declared. *The system does.*

She smiled, took a deep breath, and gave me a hug. Buoyed by the knowledge that she was not alone, it seemed, at least momentarily, that she might be able to keep swimming.

As we reimagine leadership, know this: likeability will not make or break you.

Laura, who for years was told she was not enough, finally found a workplace where her contributions were recognized and valued. In fact, she was able to convince her new boss to allocate funding that enabled her to launch a visionary project. Michelle, who was told she was too much, left the office where she was passed over for a promotion and accepted a leadership role in a new office. She turned into the superstar she knew she was, and even more doors began to open for her. Laura and Michelle understood the value they brought to their work; they just needed to find somewhere that understood it as well as they did.

I've also watched this likeability and success question play out with women whose lives are much more public than Laura's or Michelle's.

In 2012, Ellen Pao sued Kleiner Perkins Caufield & Byers, the Silicon Valley venture capital firm where she worked as a junior investing partner, for gender discrimination. By the time the case went to trial in 2015, it became a public referendum on Pao's likeability. In testimony from former colleagues, Pao was described as "kind of a downer," "not a warm and fuzzy person," and "entitled."

Who could forget Anne Hathaway's 2013 Academy Award acceptance speech for best supporting actress? The Hatha-haters came out swinging, with more words dedicated to dissecting her persona than there are think pieces on millennial entitlement. Howard Stern declared, "Everyone sort of hates Anne Hathaway" and the *San Francisco Chronicle* crowned her "The Most Annoying Celebrity of 2013." Yet few of her critics seemed to question the actual quality of her acting.

And then there is Hillary Clinton, who has had to defend her likeability more often than I've had to brush my own hair. During the 2008 presidential election, onstage at the ABC News–Facebook–WMUR New Hampshire Democratic primary debate, a moderator asked Clinton, "What can you say to the voters of New Hampshire on this stage tonight who see a résumé and like it, but are hesitating on the likeability issue, where they seem to like Barack Obama more?" Imagine being asked that question in your own life. "So, Alicia, we'd really like to give you this promotion. You're a really hard worker! Your résumé is stellar! So much experience! But everyone just *likes* José more!"

The question itself was rough, but as if to add insult to injury, then Senator Barack Obama quipped, "You're likeable enough, Hillary." (Ironically, that backhanded compliment was generally viewed as a moment in which the ordinarily affable Obama seemed less likeable.)

I don't know Pao, Hathaway, or Clinton personally (though I've met and interviewed Clinton on several occasions). But I'm intrigued that rather than focus exclusively on their results, their impact on the bottom line, or their actual talents, they were all instead described by their perceived demeanor. And I'm struck by the price, however big or small, they've each paid for being thought of as unlikeable.

In a personal essay for *Lenny Letter*, Pao described the complexity of navigating sexism in the tech world, writing, "Am I really too ambitious while being too quiet while being too aggressive while being unlikeable?"

In an interview with *InStyle* magazine, Hathaway described the public scrutiny she endured as "being hunted" and admitted that it made her "very unhappy."

And Clinton's response to that question on likeability? "Well, that hurts my feelings."

Yet all of those women survived.

After a jury decided Pao's case in favor of her former employer, Pao went on to join Reddit as the head of business development and strategic partnerships, before becoming the website's interim CEO. And even after her complicated departure from that post, Pao signed up to write a tell-all about the "toxic culture" of Silicon Valley.

Hathahaters be damned, *The Intern*, the 2015 comedy that Hathaway starred in opposite Robert De Niro, drew a whopping $194.6 million at the box office. *Ocean's 8*, the 2018 all-female heist blockbuster, made $297.7 million.

In 2016, Hillary Clinton became the first woman in history to win the presidential nomination of a major American political party, a fact that is understandably obscured by her general election loss, but a stunning achievement nonetheless.

At the beginning of this book I told you how much it matters to me that you like me. That is not as true today as it was even when I wrote those words. But the desire to be liked is an instinct, one on which much of my theory of human interaction is based, a muscle memory, and so the process of unlearning it is challenging, and slow. What is more important than learning to let that go is creating a culture where women are seen by others as leaders, see themselves as leaders, and are given opportunities to lead, just as they are. Ambitious, complicated, nice, aggressive, bossy, effective leaders.

Besides, likeability isn't a zero-sum game. Maybe it's okay to be likeable enough. Look at the achievements of the women I just mentioned, and consider their ability to survive public scrutiny and to continue to push through to create the world they want to live in. Talk about being tough. Each of these women has been penalized for being perceived as not being likeable enough, but it didn't break them. And it will not break you.

Acknowledgments

My thanks to:

Ryan Harbage, my literary agent, for his patience and enthusiasm, and for convincing me that I could do this.

Stephanie Hitchcock, my editor, who challenged me to think bigger and then supported me in that endeavor.

Josanne Lopez, my manager, who believed long before anyone else believed.

Lauren Leeds and Veronica Bautista, my friends and early readers, for their insights and for encouraging my bad jokes.

Rachel Simmons, whose own work deeply influenced my thinking and affirmed that this topic was, in fact, important.

Juleyka Lantigua-Williams, who constantly reminds me of what is possible when we "get out of line."

Ileana Ferreras, who asks all the right questions.

Thank you to all of the women who trusted me with their stories, and connected me with the women in their lives who then trusted me with theirs. This book literally could not exist without them.

I wrote this book over the course of two pregnancies, multiple job transitions, and hundreds of thousands of miles of air travel. The product of that hard work is in your hands, but the love and labor that made it achievable are not mine alone. For that, my love and thanks to my parents, Jane and Bob, my brother Rob and sister-in-law Alex, my in-laws Marián and César, my stepfather Tony, and Norma and Betty, our circle of support. Thank you for making this and all things possible.

And of course Carlos, the best husband, coparent, and late-night editor I could ask for. If I write another book, I promise to learn how to use hyphens.

Notes

Chapter 1: Please Like Me

11 hold less than 23 percent of the seats on corporate boards: "Missing Pieces Report: The 2018 Board Diversity Census of Women and Minorities on Fortune 500 Boards," Alliance for Board Diversity, January 16, 2019, 18.

11 Among the directors of the 100 top-grossing movies of 2017: Claire Cain Miller, Kevin Quealy, and Margot Sanger-Katz, "The Top Jobs Where Women Are Outnumbered by Men Named John," *New York Times*, April 24, 2018, https://www.nytimes.com/interactive/2018/04/24/upshot/women -and-men-named-john.html.

11 fewer than 1 percent of Fortune 500 companies: Dion Rabouin, "Only 1 Fortune 500 company is headed by a woman of color," *Axios*, January 14, 2019, https://www.axios.com/fortune-500-no-women-of-color-ceos -3d42619c-967b-47d2-b94c-659527b22ee3.html.

11 The thing that feels the most amorphous: *Barriers and Bias: The Status of Women in Leadership*, a report by the American Association of University Women (2016), https://www.aauw.org/aauw_check/pdf_download /show_pdf.php?file=barriers-and-bias.

11 The constant trade-offs between competence and likeability: Andrea Kupfer Schneider, Catherine H. Tinsley, Sandra Cheldelin, and Emily T. Amanatullah, "Likeability v Competence: The Impossible Choice Faced by

Female Politicians Attenuated by Lawyers," *Duke Journal of Gender and Law Policy* 17 (2010): 363–84.

12   And plenty of women, sensing that they cannot win in a male-dominated: Scott A. Moss, "Women Choosing Diverse Workplaces: A Rational Preference with Disturbing Implications for Both Occupational Segregation and Economic Analysis of Law," *Harvard Women's Law Journal* 27, no. 1 (2004), https://ssrn.com/abstract=761744.

13   Neuroticism is about confidence: For an overview of the Big Five, see Oliver P. John and Sanjay Srivastava, "The Big Five Trait taxonomy: History, measurement, and theoretical perspectives," in L. A. Pervin and O. P. John, eds, *Handbook of Personality: Theory and Research*, 2nd ed. (New York: Guilford Press, 2001) 102–38, available online: https://pages.uoregon.edu /sanjay/pubs/bigfive.pdf.

13   Studies have found a correlation between people who are extroverted: Thomas Lösch and Katrin Rentzsch, "Linking Personality with Interpersonal Perception in the Classroom: Distinct Associations with the Social and Academic Sides of Popularity," *Journal of Research in Personality* 75 (August 2018): 83–93, https://doi.org/10.1016/j.jrp.2018.06.003.

13   Popularity is about status: Mitch Prinstein, *Popular: Why Being Liked Is the Secret to Greater Success and Happiness* (New York: Viking, 2017).

14   Making other people feel important: Dale Carnegie, *How to Win Friends and Influence People* (New York: Simon & Schuster, 2009).

18   As Mitch Prinstein writes: Prinstein, *Popular*, 4.

21   I focused largely on ambitious, professional: I have no doubt that working-class women contend with these issues, but for them, being likeable comes into conflict as much with survival as with success. Most of the research I found on likeability and perceptions of strength and warmth within organizations use frameworks such as "middle-management" and "performance reviews" that seem to imagine a worker who is at least middle-class, and upwardly mobile. The research on bias and stereotypes notes that the poor are often stereotyped as cold and incompetent, eliciting contempt. While those researchers apply the term more broadly, one can imagine that those perceptions often replicate in low-wage workplaces. More anecdotally, if you are working retail sales or a food service job, how well liked you are may determine something critical to economic survival, such as how many shifts your employer grants you. Some of the terrain, such as likeability in hiring and in promotions, is undoubtedly the same for working-class women and professional women, and some of it, such as identifying a predatory manager or unsafe work practices, is more risky for women with less education and economic power.

Chapter 2: The Goldilocks Conundrum

24   Laura is in her mid-thirties: You'll notice that some of these women allowed me to use their names, and others asked me to conceal their identity. In some cases, where anonymity was requested, I have collapsed several women together to create a composite.

30   "My kids keep asking how many times we have to win": Tamar Lewin, "Partnership in Firm Awarded to Victim of Sex Discrimination," *New York Times*, May 16, 1990, https://www.nytimes.com/1990/05/16/us /partnership-in-firm-awarded-to-victim-of-sex-bias.html; Andrea Sachs, "A Slap at Sex Stereotypes," *Time*, June 24, 2001, http://content.time.com /time/magazine/article/0,9171,151787,00.html; Gillian Thomas, *Because of Sex: One Law, Ten Cases, and Fifty Years That Changed American Women's Lives at Work* (New York: St. Martin's Press, 2016).

31   In many cases, covert discrimination at work: Eden Kind and Kristen Jones, "Why Subtle Bias Is So Often Worse than Blatant Discrimination," *Harvard Business Review*, July 13, 2016.

31   Hopkins's coworkers turned friends: Tamar Lewin, "Winner of Sex Bias Suit Set to Enter New Arena," *New York Times*, May 19, 1990, https:// www.nytimes.com/1990/05/19/us/winner-of-sex-bias-suit-set-to-enter -next-arena.html.

32   Read: you can purport to be "super woke": For an overview on the research on unconscious/implicit bias: Anthony G. Greenwald and Linda Hamilton Krieger, "Implicit Bias: Scientific Foundations," *California Law Review* 94, no. 4, 2006, https://doi.org/10.15779/Z38GH7F. See also: Cheryl Staats, "State of the Science: Implicit Bias Review 2013," Kirwan Institute, Ohio State University, 2013, https://cdn.ymaws.com/www.napaba.org /resource/resmgr/2016_napaba_con/CLE_Materials/CLE_WLN2.pdf.

32   Analysis by Catalyst: *What Is Unconscious Bias?* New York: Catalyst, December 11, 2014.

33   pinpointed two qualities that form the basis of our judgments: Researchers disagree over what to call these traits (some use "competence" rather than "strength"), but agree that they are the primary dimensions we use to assess others. While there is much research on this topic, I was first introduced to the topic by, and thus my primary understanding of it is based on the work of, John Neffinger and Matthew Kohut, and their work with Amy Cuddy. See: Matthew Kohut and John Neffinger, *Compelling People: The Hidden Qualities That Make Us Influential* (New York: Hudson Street Press, 2013); Susan T. Fiske, Amy J. C. Cuddy, and Peter Glick, "Universal Dimensions of Social Cognition: Warmth and Competence," *Trends in Cognitive Science* 11, no. 2 (February 2007): 77–83, https://doi.org/10.1016/j .tics.2006.11.005; Amy J. C. Cuddy, Susan T. Fiske, and Peter Glick, "Warmth

and Competence as Universal Dimensions of Social Perception: The Stereotype Content Model and the BIAS Map," *Advances in Experimental Social Psychology* 40 (2008) 61–149, https://doi.org/10.1016/S0065-2601(07)00002-0; Amy J. C. Cuddy, Peter Glick, and Anna Beninger, "The Dynamics of Warmth and Competence Judgments, and Their Outcomes in Organizations," *Research in Organizational Behavior* 31 (2011): 73–98, https://doi.org/10.1016/j.riob.2011.10.004; Amy J. C. Cuddy, Susan T. Fiske, and Peter Glick, "The BIAS Map: Behaviors from Intergroup Affect and Stereotypes," *Journal of Personality and Social Psychology* 92, no. 4 (2007): 631–648, http://dx.doi.org/10.1037/0022-3514.92.4.631; Susan T. Fiske, Amy J. C. Cuddy, Peter Glick, and Jun Xu, " A Model of (Often Mixed) Stereotype Content: Competence and Warmth Respectively Follow from Perceived Status and Competition," *Journal of Personality and Social Psychology* 82, no. 6 (2002): 878–902; Charles M. Judd, Laurie James-Hawkins, Vincent Yzerbyt, and Yoshihisa Kashima, "Fundamental Dimensions of Social Judgment: Understanding the Relations Between Judgments of Competence and Warmth," *Journal of Personality and Social Psychology* 89, no. 6 (2005): 899–913.

34 But these judgments are often informed: Cuddy, Fiske, and Glick, "Warmth and Competence as Universal Dimensions of Social Perception."

35 Conversely, if that coworker describes you as: Nicolas Kervyn, Hilary B. Bergsieker, and Susan T. Fiske, "The Innuendo Effect: Hearing the Positive but Inferring the Negative," *Journal of Experimental Social Psychology* 48, no. 1 (January 2012): 77–85.

35 A new client, a new win, or setting a new record: Cuddy, Glick, and Beninger, "The Dynamics of Warmth and Competence Judgments, and their Outcomes in Organizations," 17.

36 If she is assertive and direct: There is so much incredible research on women, agency, and backlash. Several works stand out to me as the must-reads on this topic. See Laurie A. Rudman, "Self-Promotion as a Risk Factor for Women: The Costs and Benefits of Counterstereotypical Impression Management," *Journal of Personality and Social Psychology* 74 (1998): 629–45.

Chapter 3: Likeability and Authenticity as Luxuries

45 In the first line of her piece Stanley writes: Alessandra Stanley, "Wrought in Rhimes' Image," *New York Times*, September 18, 2014. https://www.nytimes.com/2014/09/21/arts/television/viola-davis-plays-shonda-rhimess-latest-tough-heroine.html.

45 Stanley insisted in the aftermath: Jaimie Etkin, "Shonda Rhimes Fires Back at the Critic Who Called Her an 'Angry Black Woman,'" Buzzfeed News, September 19, 2014, https://www.buzzfeednews.com/article/jaimie etkin/shonda-rhimes-response-to-angry-black-woman#3i2tbe8.

45 But most commenters did not see it that way: Shonda Rhimes, Twitter post, September 19, 2014, 7:24 a.m., https://twitter.com/shondarhimes /status/512970400083750912.

46 "I feel like people think I'm mean": Rob Haskell, "Serena Williams on Pregnancy, Power and Coming Back to Center Court," *Vogue*, August 15, 2017.

47 Under this model, scholars argue: Robert W. Livingston and Ashleigh Shelby Rosette, "Failure Is Not an Option for Black Women: Effects of Organizational Performance on Leaders with Single Versus Dual-Subordinate Identities," *Journal of Experimental Social Psychology* 48, no. 5 (September 2012): 1162–67, https://doi.org/10.1016/j.jesp.2012.05.002.

47 And there is also research that suggests: Robert W. Livingston, Ashleigh Shelby Rosette, and Ella F. Washington, "Can an Agentic Black Woman Get Ahead? The Impact of Race and Interpersonal Dominance on Perceptions of Female Leaders," *Psychological Science* 23, no. 4, (March 2012): 354–58, https://doi.org/10.1177/0956797611428079.

48 Perhaps worse, a black woman who strives to lead: Sylvia Ann Hewlett and Tai Wingfield, "Qualified Black Women Are Being Held Back from Management," *Harvard Business Review*, June 11, 2015.

48 She was called "angry" and "aggressive": Ben Smith, "Court Tapes Show Blunt Sotomayor," *Politico*, July, 17, 2009, https://www.politico.com /story/2009/07/court-tapes-show-blunt-sotomayor-025087.

48 Following Sotomayor's dissent: Sahil Kapur, "Conservatives Rip into Sotomayor's 'Legally Illiterate' Dissent on Race," Talking Points Memo, April 23, 2014. https://talkingpointsmemo.com/dc/sonia-sotomayor -race-conservatives.

48 Recent analysis of Harvard's admissions: Anemona Hartocollis, "Harvard Rated Asian-American Applicants Lower on Personality Traits," *New York Times*, June 15, 2018, https://www.nytimes.com/2018/06/15/us /harvard-asian-enrollment-applicants.html.

48 Yet that perception of competence: Joan C. Williams, Marina Multhaup, and Rachel Korn, "The Problem with 'Asians Are Good at Science,'" *Atlantic*, January 31, 2018, https://www.theatlantic.com/science /archive/2018/01/asian-americans-science-math-bias/551903/.

49 One study of Bay Area technology companies: Buck Gee and Denise Peck, "The Illusion of Asian Success: Scant Progress for Minorities in Cracking the Glass Ceiling from 2007–2015," report by the Ascend Foundation, 2017.

49 One study found that given the choice: Jennifer L. Berdahl and Ji-A Min, "Prescriptive Stereotypes and Workplace Consequences for East Asians

in North America," *Cultural Diversity and Ethnic Minority Psychology* 18, no. 2 (2012): 141–52.

49 So those women are under enormous pressure: Adam D. Galinsky, Erika V. Hall, and Amy J. C. Cuddy, "Gendered Races: Implications for Interracial Marriage, Leadership Selection, and Athletic Participation," *Psychological Science* 24, no. 4 (March 8, 2013): 498–506, https://doi.org/10.1177/0956797612457783.

50 The *Washington Post* called the West Wing: Juliet Eilperin, "White House Women Want to Be in the Room Where It Happens," *Washington Post*, September 13, 2016, https://www.washingtonpost.com/news/powerpost/wp/2016/09/13/white-house-women-are-now-in-the-room-where-it-happens/?utm_term=.e9c427cb0f75.

52 They are twice as likely as white LGBTQ: NPR/Robert Wood Johnson Foundation/Harvard T. H. Chan School of Public Health, "Discrimination in America: Experience and Views of LGBTQ Americans," November 2017, https://cdn1.sph.harvard.edu/wp-content/uploads/sites/94/2017/11/NPR-RWJF-HSPH-Discrimination-LGBTQ-Final-Report.pdf.

53 LGBTQ workers are more likely to be told: Deena Fidas, "The Cost of the Closet and the Rewards of Inclusion: Why the Workplace Environment for LGBTQ People Matters to Employers," report by the Human Rights Campaign Foundation, May 2014.

56 But when it came to questions of competence: Madeline Heilman and Tyler Okimoto, "Motherhood: A Potential Source of Bias in Employment Decisions," *Journal of Applied Psychology* 93 (February 2008): 189–98.

57 Another study found that in addition to the competence demerit: Shelley J. Correll, Stephen Benard, and In Paik, "Getting a Job: Is There a Motherhood Penalty?" *American Journal of Sociology* 112, no. 5 (2007): 1297–338, doi:10.1086/511799.

57 In one experiment, researchers created a series of videos: Cathy Tinsley et al., Should I Stay or Should I Go? Gender, Work-life Crisis, and Predictability, 2008, unpublished working paper, on file http://guwli.georgetown.edu/research; Via Schneider, Tinsley, Cheldelin, and Amanatullah, "Likeability v. Competence: The Impossible Choice Faced by Female Politicians Attenuated by Lawyers," 2010.

58 Eighty-three percent of: Kenji Yoshino and Christie Smith, "Uncovering Talent: A New Model of Inclusion," Deloitte, December 6, 2013; "What Is Covering?" Catalyst, New York, December 11, 2014.

61 Sidney Madden, an NPR editor, dubbed the velocity: Sidney Madden, "The Business of Being Cardi B," NPR, April 5, 2018, https://www.npr.org/sections/therecord/2018/04/05/599592959/the-business-of-being-cardi-b.

Chapter 4: Damned If You Do

70 In contrast, people liked Howard just fine: "Gender-Related Material in the New Core Curriculum: To Attendees at the WIM Banquet," January 1, 2007, from Professor Joanne Martin," 2017, https://www.gsb.stanford.edu /experience/news-history/gender-related-material-new-core-curriculum.

71 When competent women apply for a job: Julie E. Phelan, Corinne A. Moss-Racusin, and Laurie A. Rudman, "Competent Yet Out in the Cold: Shifting Criteria for Hiring Reflect Backlash Toward Agentic Women," *Psychology of Women Quarterly* 32, no. 4 (December 1, 2008), 406–13, https:// doi.org/10.1111/j.1471-6402.2008.00454.x.

72 Among math majors, male applicants: Natasha Quadlin, "The Mark of a Woman's Record: Gender and Academic Performance in Hiring the Mark of a Woman's Record," *American Sociological Review* 83, no. 2 (March 15, 2018): 331–60, https://doi.org/10.1177/0003122418762291.

72 "Their comments suggest that when women": Ibid., 349.

74 And they pay a real price for that: Laurie A. Rudman, "Self-Promotion as a Risk Factor for Women: The Costs and Benefits of Counterstereotypical Impression Management," *Journal of Personality and Social Psychology* 74 (1998): 629–45. See also Ronnie Janoff-Bulman and Mary Beth Wade, "Viewpoint: The Dilemma of Self-Advocacy for Women: Another Case of Blaming the Victim?" *Journal of Social and Clinical Psychology* 15 (1996): 143–52.

75 "On the whole these provisions indicate": "A New Kind of PFO: Mid-Negotiating, Post-Offer," Philosophy Smoker, March 11, 2014, http:// philosophysmoker.blogspot.com/2014/03/a-new-kind-of-pfo-mid-negotiating -post.html.

75 Negotiating can have big advantages: Women in the Workplace 2017, McKinsey and LeanIn.org, https://www.mckinsey.com/featured-insights /gender-equality/women-in-the-workplace-2017.

76 Much of my discomfort around asking: This idea seems to have been first introduced by Andrea Donderi, a commenter on an Ask MetaFilter post, https://ask.metafilter.com/55153/Whats-the-middle-ground-between -FU-and-Welcome#830421; Alex Eichler, "'Askers' vs. 'Guessers,'" The Wire, May 12, 2010, https://www.theatlantic.com/national/archive/2010/05 /askers-vs-guessers/340891/.

77 Women who negotiate: Women in the Workplace 2017, 10.

78 And, because women have long been considered: Hannah Riley Bowles, Linda Babcock, and Lei Lai, "Social Incentives for Gender Differences in the Propensity to Initiate Negotiations: Sometimes It Does Hurt to Ask," *Organizational Behavior and Human Decision Processes* 103 (2007): 86, https://www.cfa.harvard.edu/cfawis/bowles.pdf.

78   A simulated salary negotiation: Emily T. Amanatullah, "Negotiating Gender Role Stereotypes: The Influence of Gender Role Stereotypes on Perceivers' Evaluations and Targets' Behaviors in Value Claiming Negotiations and Situational Moderation by Representation Role" (Ph.D. diss., Columbia University, 2007), retrieved October 9, 2008, from Dissertations & Theses: Full Text Database (Publication No. AAT 3285036), 57, available at https://www8.gsb.columbia.edu/ipmedia/203/0986870f-4201-0000-0080 -8d331bb7746b/e8b98d0f-4201-0000-0080-8d331bb7746b.pdf.

79   Men asked for more than $48,000: Emily T. Amanatullah and Michael W. Morris, "Negotiating Gender Roles: Gender Differences in Assertive Negotiating Are Mediated by Women's Fear of Backlash and Attenuated When Negotiating on Behalf of Others," *Journal of Personality and Social Psychology* 98, no. 2 (2010): 256–67.

79   Simply anticipating that there will be backlash: Ibid.

79   "I got mad at myself." Jennifer Lawrence, "Why Do I Make Less Than My Male Co-Stars," *Lenny Letter*, no. 3.

80   "Are you sure you want me to?" Kaitlin Menza, "What I Wish I Said to the Recruiter Who Offered Me a Lower Salary," *Marie Claire*, March 8, 2017.

81   "This is how I thought negotiating worked": "W Speaks About Her FO," Philosophy Smoker, March 13, 2014, http://philosophysmoker.blogspot .com/2014/03/w-speaks-about-her-pfo-fo.html.

81   Women are more likely to receive critical subjective feedback: Paola Cecchi-Dimeglio, "How Gender Bias Corrupts Performance Reviews, and What to do About It," *Harvard Business Review*, April 12, 2017. See also Monica Biernat, M. J. Tocci, and Joan Williams, "The Language of Performance Evaluations: Gender-Based Shifts in Content and Consistency of Judgment," *Social Psychological and Personality Science* 3 (2012): 186–92; Madeline Heilman, " Description and Prescription: How Gender Stereotypes Prevent Women's Ascent Up the Organizational Ladder," *Journal of Social Issues* 57, no. 4 (2001): 657–74, http://dx.doi.org/10.1111/0022-4537.00234.

82   The feedback women receive is often vague: Shelley Correll and Caroline Simard, "Research: Vague Feedback Is Holding Women Back," *Harvard Business Review*, April 29, 2016, https://hbr.org/2016/04/research -vague-feedback-is-holding-women-back.

82   To mitigate the awkwardness: Lily Jampol and Vivian Zayas, "Gendered White Lies: Performance Feedback Is Upwardly Distorted to Women," April 1, 2017, available at SSRN, https://ssrn.com/abstract=2953053.

83   In Jampol's analysis: Lily Jampol, Aneeta Rattan, and Elizabeth

Baily Wolf, "A Bias Toward Kindness Goals in Performance Feedback to Women" (under review at *Psychological Science*).

83 Ursula Burns, the former CEO of Xerox: Adam Bryant, "Xerox's New Chief Tries to Redefine Its Culture," *New York Times*, February 20, 2010, https://www.nytimes.com/2010/02/21/business/21xerox.html.

84 You must be a monster: Madeline Heilman and Julie J. Chen, "Same Behavior, Different Consequences: Reactions to Men's and Women's Altruistic Citizenship Behavior," *Journal of Applied Psychology* 90 (2005): 431–41.

84 That's not because they can't focus: Ronnie Janoff-Bulman and Mary Beth Wade, "The Dilemma of Self-Advocacy for Women: Another Case of Blaming the Victim?" *Journal of Social and Clinical Psychology* 15 (1996): 143–52; Alice H. Eagly and Maureen Crowley, "Gender and Helping Behavior: A Meta-Analytic Review of the Social Psychological Literature," *Psychological Bulletin* 100 (1986): 283–308.

86 Unfortunately for Marisol and those like her: Alice Eagly and Linda L. Carli, "Women and the Labyrinth of Leadership," *Harvard Business Review*, September 2007, https://hbr.org/2007/09/women-and-the-labyrinth-of-leadership.

87 regarded men and women leaders in much the same way: "Women and Leadership: Public Says Women Are Equally Qualified, but Barriers Persist," Washington, D.C., Pew Research Center, January 2015, http://www.pewsocialtrends.org/2015/01/14/women-and-leadership/.

87 And women, especially younger women: Ibid.

88 Sounds wildly selfish to me!: Sylvia Ann Hewlett and Tai Green, "Black Women Ready to Lead," a report by the Center for Talent Innovation, 2015. See also "Women in the Workplace 2017."

Chapter 5: The Power Grab

91 "Super unlikable": "Trump vs. Clinton: Trump Is a Super-Unlikable Candidate," *Pacific Standard*, October 9, 2016, https://psmag.com/news/trump-vs-clinton-trump-is-a-super-unlikable-candidate.

91 "likeability epidemic": Chris Cillizza, "Hillary Clinton Has a Likeability Problem. Donald Trump Has a Llikeability Epidemic," *Washington Post*, May 16, 2016, https://www.washingtonpost.com/news/the-fix/wp/2016/05/16/hillary-clintons-long-lingering-likeable-enough-problem/?utm_term=.72c8a28d2d5c.

91 "Why do so many people hate Ted Cruz?": Nick Allen, "Why Do So Many People Hate Ted Cruz," *Telegraph*, January 26, 2016, http://www.

.telegraph.co.uk/news/worldnews/us-politics/12121499/Why-do-so-many
-people-hate-Ted-Cruz.html.

92 "malfunctioning robot" and a "disagreeable human being": Mi-chael Brendan Dougherty, "Mitt Romney Is a Total Disaster and There's a Simple Explanation Why," *Business Insider*, December 2, 2011, http://www
.businessinsider.com/mitt-romney-is-a-total-disaster-and-theres-a-simple
-explanation-2011-12.

92 "aloof" and "emotionless": David Rohde, "How John Kerry Could End Up Outdoing Hillary Clinton," *Atlantic*, December 2013, https://www
.theatlantic.com/magazine/archive/2013/12/john-kerry-will-not-be
-denied/354688/.

92 "know it all," "wooden," and "stiff": William Schneider, "Al Gore's Problem," *National Journal*, December 2, 2011, http://www.uvm.edu
/~dguber/POLS125/articles/schneider.htm.

92 Her opponents called the Democratic politician: Mark Z. Barabak, "Triumph of the 'Airhead,'" *Los Angeles Times*, January 26, 2003, https://
www.latimes.com/archives/la-xpm-2003-jan-26-tm-pelosi4-story.html.

93 And on top of all that, voters like when a woman: "Politics Is Personal: Keys to Likeability and Electability for Women," Barbara Lee Family Foundation research memo, April 2016.

93 It doesn't matter whether the coverage is positive: Rachel Joy Larries and Rosalie Maggio, "Name It, Change It. The Women's Media Center's Guide to Gender Neutral Coverage of Women Candidates + Politicians," Women's Media Center (2012): 4, https://wmc.3cdn.net/b2d5a7532d50091943
_n1m6b1avk.pdf.

93 In one experimental survey: "Name It, Change It: An Examination of the Impact of Media Coverage of Women Candidates' Appearance," Women's Media Center and She Should Run, 2010, http://www.nameitchangeit.org
/page/-/Name-It-Change-It-Executive-Summary-Appearance-Research.pdf.

94 Newer research has found that voters: "Politics Is Personal: Keys to Likeability and Electability for Women," 2.

95 "For male candidates, being authentically male": Kelly Dittmar, "On the Bias 9.7.15," Presidential Gender Watch 2016, a project of the Barbara Lee Family Foundation and the Center for American Women in Politics, September 7, 2015, http://presidentialgenderwatch.org/on-the-bias-9-7-15
/#more-3798.

97 The panel cleared her of wrongdoing: Carey Goldberg, "Ethics Ruling Faults Massachusetts Official," *New York Times*, August 24, 2000, https://
www.nytimes.com/2000/08/24/us/ethics-ruling-faults-massachusetts
-official.html.

97 Professor Susan Carroll sums it up: Michael Alison Chandler, "More Mothers of Young Kids Are Running for Political Office," *Washington Post*, November 1, 2017.

97 Women candidates, when questioned about their family: "Modern Family: How Women Candidates Can Talk About Politics, Parenting, and Their Personal Lives," Barbara Lee Family Foundation, 2017, http://oe9e 345wags3x5qikp6dg012.wpengine.netdna-cdn.com/wp-content/uploads /BL_Memo_Final-3.22.17.pdf.

98 A poll showed Romney: Mitch Frank, "Jane Swift Takes One for the Team," *Time*, March 21, 2002, http://content.time.com/time/nation /article/0,8599,219417,00.html.

99 A 2013 anonymous poll: Ed Vogel, "Poll Ranks Best, Worst Legislators," *Las Vegas Review-Journal*, June 9, 2013, https://www.reviewjournal .com/news/politics-and-government/nevada/poll-ranks-best-worst-legislators -in-nevada/.

101 A former New York public advocate: Michael M. Grynbaum and David W. Chen, "Offstage, Quinn Isn't Afraid to Let Fury Fly," *New York Times*, March 25, 2013, http://www.nytimes.com/2013/03/26/nyregion /in-private-quinn-displays-a-volatile-side.html.

101 In a post-election analysis piece: Jodi Kantor and Kate Taylor, "In Quinn's Loss, Questions About Role of Gender and Sexuality," *New York Times*, September 11, 2013, https://www.nytimes.com/2013/09/12 /nyregion/in-quinns-loss-questions-about-role-of-gender-and-sexuality .html?pagewanted=print.

102 But even with the full context, provided by the de Blasio campaign: Joe Coscarelli, "Maureen Dowd's Frankenstein Quote Gave Christine Quinn a Temporary Opening on de Blasio," *New York*, Aug 21, 2013, http://nymag .com/intelligencer/2013/08/maureen-dowd-misquote-gave-quinn-an-opening .html.

102 The same research that detailed voters' concerns: "Modern Family: How Women Candidates Can Talk About Politics, Parenting, and Their Personal Lives," Barbara Lee Family Foundation, 2017.

105 "You don't have to like her": "Oprah Endorses Hillary Clinton on TD Jakes Show," T. D. Jakes, October 21, 2016, https://www.wtsp.com /video/entertainment/television/programs/td-jakes/oprah-endorses-hillary -clinton-on-td-jakes-show/85-2399408.

106 "If I ever entertained the idea of voting for Bill Clinton": Denver Nicks, "The Hillary Clinton Comment That Sparked Lena Dunham's Political Awareness," *Time*, September 29, 2015, http://time.com/4054623/clinton -dunham-tea-cookies/.

107 "I actually have emotions": "Clinton: 'I Actually Have Emotions,'" CNN, January 8, 2008, http://politicalticker.blogs.cnn.com/2008/01/08/clinton-i-actually-have-emotions/.

107 In fact, her favorability among Republicans: Andrew Dugan and Justin McCarthy, "Hillary Clinton's Favorable Rating One of Her Worst," Gallup, September 4, 2015, https://news.gallup.com/poll/185324/hillary-clinton-favorable-rating-one-worst.aspx.

107 "Once I moved from serving someone": Rebecca Traister, "Hillary Clinton Is Furious. And Resigned. And Funny. And Worried. The Surreal Post-Election Life of the Woman Who Would Have Been President," *New York*, May 29, 2017.

109 In fact, his transparent desire for power: Tyler G. Okimoto and Victoria Brescoll, "The Price of Power: Power Seeking and Backlash Against Female Politicians," *Personality and Social Psychology Bulletin* 36, no. 7 (2010): 923–36, doi:10.1177/0146167210371949.

Chapter 6: Public Person; Private Self

117 "Ann has been crushed by this": Lewin, "Winner of Sex Bias Suit to Enter Next Arena."

120 Men are somewhat more likely than women: Monica Anderson, "Key Takeaways on How Americans View—and Experience—Online Harassment," Pew Research Center, July 11, 2017, http://www.pewresearch.org/fact-tank/2017/07/11/key-takeaways-online-harassment/.

120 Women with public profiles: "Amnesty Reveals Alarming Impact of Online Abuse Against Women," Amnesty International, November 20, 2017, https://www.amnesty.org/en/latest/news/2017/11/amnesty-reveals-alarming-impact-of-online-abuse-against-women/.

120 Women use Facebook more than men: Shannon Greenwood, Andrew Perrin, and Maeve Duggan, "Social Media Update 2016," Pew Research Center, November 11, 2016, http://www.pewinternet.org/2016/11/11/social-media-update-2016/.

120 "Social media rewards behaviors": Rachel Simmons, *Enough as She Is: How to Help Girls Move Beyond Impossible Standards of Success to Live Happy, Healthy, and Fulfilling Lives* (New York: HarperCollins, 2018).

125 "I'm done with that": Charlotte Alter, "Are You There Angela Merkel? It's Me, Hillary!" *Time*, June 11, 2014, http://time.com/2853811/are-you-there-angela-merkel-its-me-hillary/.

125 "They say you are not you except": Robert Penn Warren, *All the King's Men* (New York: Chelsea House, 1987).

126 "The whole thing, with the attacks from everything": Dan Zak,

"Ann Romney Can Feel Hillary Clinton's Pain," *Washington Post*, October 8, 2015, https://www.washingtonpost.com/lifestyle/style/ann-romney-can -feel-hillary-rodham-clintons-pain/2015/10/08/4de781fc-6c4e-11e5-9bfe -e59f5e244f92_story.html?utm_term=.9eb725348d83.

126 "Barack is very much human": "Your Next First Lady," *Glamour*, September 3, 2007.

Chapter 7: Angry Women Everywhere

130 "Look at that face": Paul Solotaroff, "Trump Seriously: On the Trail with the GOP's Tough Guy," *Rolling Stone*, September 9, 2015, https://www .rollingstone.com/politics/politics-news/trump-seriously-on-the-trail-with -the-gops-tough-guy-41447/.

131 "All my life I had worked hard": Carly Fiorina, *Tough Choices* (New York: Penguin Group, 2006), 54.

134 "She's a bitch but he's just having a bad day": Lisa F. Barrett and Eliza Bliss-Moreau, "She's Emotional. He's Having a Bad Day: Attributional Explanations for Emotion Stereotypes," *Emotion* 9, no. 5 (2009): 649–58, http://dx.doi.org/10.1037/a0016821. See also Lisa F. Barrett, "Hillary Clinton's Angry Face," *New York Times*, September 23, 2016, https://www.ny times.com/2016/09/25/opinion/sunday/hillary-clintons-angry-face.html.

134 Writer Jessica Bennett describes RBF: Jessica Bennett, "I'm Not Mad. That's Just My RBF," *New York Times*, August 1, 2015, https://www .nytimes.com/2015/08/02/fashion/im-not-mad-thats-just-my-resting-b -face.html.

134 But for black men who seek positions of power: Robert W. Livingston and Nicholas A. Pearce, "The Teddy-Bear Effect: Does Having a Baby Face Benefit Black Chief Executive Officers?" *Psychological Science* 20, no. 10 (October 2009): 1229–36, https://doi.org/10.1111/j.1467-9280.2009.02431.x.

134 While there's little you can do about your face: Victoria L. Brescoll and Eric Luis Uhlmann, "Can an Angry Woman Get Ahead? Status Conferral, Gender, and Expression of Emotion in the Workplace," *Psychological Science* 19, no. 3, (2008): 268–75, https://doi.org/10.1111/j.1467 -9280.2008.02079.x.

135 Her anger made her less persuasive: Jessica M. Salerno, Liana C. Peter-Hagene, and Alexander C. V. Jay, "Women and African Americans Are Less Influential When They Express Anger During Group Decision Making," *Group Processes and Intergroup Relations* 1, no. 23 (2017): 1–23.

136 They are perceived as more competent: Larissa Z. Tiedens, "Anger and Advancement Versus Sadness and Subjugation: The Effect of Negative Emotion Expressions on Social Status Conferral," *Journal of Personality and Social Psychology* 80 (2001) 86–94. See also Brescoll and Uhlmann, "Can

an Angry Woman Get Ahead? Status Conferral, Gender, and Expression of Emotion in the Workplace," 273.

138 Those books—none more than *Lean In*: Erin Durkin, "Michelle Obama on 'Leaning In': 'Sometimes That Shit Doesn't Work,'" *Guardian*, December 3, 2018, https://www.theguardian.com/us-news/2018/dec/03 /michelle-obama-lean-in-sheryl-sandberg.

Chapter 8: Addressing the Emotional Cost

148 She claimed that women were: Susan Nolen-Hoeksema, *Women Who Think Too Much: How to Break Free of Overthinking and Reclaim Your Life* (New York: St. Martin's Griffin, 2003), 3.

149 This is what Nolen-Hoeksema called: Ibid., 9.

156 This type of guide is particularly important: Stacy Blake-Beard, Audrey Murrell, and David Thomas, "Unfinished Business: The Impact of Race on Understanding Mentoring Relationships," Harvard Business School Working Paper, No. 06-060, June 2006.

156 In her book *Forget a Mentor, Find a Sponsor*: Sylvia Ann Hewlett, *Forget a Mentor, Find a Sponsor: The New Way to Fast Track Your Career* (Boston: Harvard Business School Publishing, 2013).

157 To find a sponsor: Ibid.

157 In targeting a would-be sponsor: Dan Schawbel, "Sylvia Ann Hewlett: Find a Sponsor Instead of a Mentor," *Forbes*, September 10, 2013, https:// www.forbes.com/sites/danschawbel/2013/09/10/sylvia-ann-hewlett-find-a -sponsor-instead-of-a-mentor/#48cb2db11760.

165 "the world's largest and indisputably weirdest": Kevin Roose, "Pursuing Self-Interest in Harmony with the Laws of the Universe and Contributing to Evolution Is Universally Rewarded," *New York*, April 10, 2011, http://nymag.com/news/business/wallstreet/ray-dalio-2011-4/.

165 a "cauldron of fear and intimidation": Alexandra Stevenson and Matthew Goldstein, "At World's Largest Hedge Fund, Sex, Fear and Video Surveillance," *New York Times*, July 26, 2016.

165 "unusual and confrontational": Alexandra Stevenson and Matthew Goldstein, "Bridgewater's Ray Dalio Spreads His Gospel of Radical Transparency," *New York Times*, September 8, 2017.

Chapter 9: Shifting Away from Likeability

169 Reese Witherspoon says she is "allergic": Reese Witherspoon, "We Have to Change the Idea That a Woman with Ambition Is Out Only for Herself," *Glamour*, September 15, 2017.

169 "We don't want Reese to say profanity.": Cara Buckley, "No More Ms. Nice Gal," *New York Times*, October 29, 2014, https://www.nytimes.com/2014/11/02/movies/reese-witherspoon-goes-against-type-in-wild.html?smid=tw-nytimes&_r=0.

170 In 2015, she gave a speech at *Glamour*'s Woman of the Year awards: Anna Moeslein, "Reese Witherspoon's Moving Speech at Glamour's 2015 Women of the Year Awards: 'Like Elle Woods, I Do Not Like to be Underestimated,'" *Glamour*, November 9. 2015, https://www.glamour.com/story/reese-witherspoon-women-of-the-year-speech.

171 She was leaving a high-level job at Nike: Mindy Grossman, "HSN's CEO on Fixing the Shopping Network's Culture," *Harvard Business Review*, December 2011, https://hbr.org/2011/12/hsns-ceo-on-fixing-the-shopping-networks-culture.

172 By 2016, the company was earning: Ellen Byron and Joann S. Lublin, "HSN's Grossman to Take Reins at Weight Watchers," *Wall Street Journal*, April 26, 2017, https://www.wsj.com/articles/hsns-grossman-to-take-reins-at-weight-watchers-1493246093.

176 Sometimes, the things we need to do: J. Crocker, M. A. Olivier, and N. Nuer, "Self-Image Goals and Compassionate Goals: Costs and Benefits," *Self Identity* 8, nos. 2–3 (2009): 251–69, doi:10.1080/15298860802505160.

177 In 2012 I interviewed Mindy Kaling: "Mindy Kaling in Conversation with Alicia Menendez," Women in the World, YouTube, April 7, 2016, https://www.youtube.com/watch?v=9wjDbqFIuhY.

178 Once asked about the divisive nature: Denise Martin, "Shonda Rhimes Talks *Scandal*'s Brutal Season 3 and the Issue of likeability," *Vulture*, December 6, 2013.

Chapter 10: What We Can Do, as Individuals and as Organizations

184 Natalia is a self-identified cis queer Latina: Natalia Oberti Noguera, interview by Alicia Menendez, *Latina to Latina*, May 1, 2018.

185 If so, Catalyst offers a variety: Catalyst, Flip the Script: Women in the Workplace (May 7, 2018), https://www.catalyst.org/research/flip-the-script-women-in-the-workplace/.

185 The Time's Up Plus One Initiative: Kristine Liao, "How Event Guests Can Make an Impact with a Plus One," BizBash, July 26, 2018, https://www.bizbash.com/experiential/article/13233881/how-event-guests-can-make-an-impact-with-a-plus-one.

186 Research shows that while executives in general: David R. Hekman, Stefanie K. Johnson, Maw-Der Foo, and Wei Yang, "Does Diversity-Valuing

Behavior Result in Diminished Performance Ratings for Non-White and Female Leaders?" *Academy of Management Journal* 60, no. 2 (March 2016), https://doi.org/10.5465/amj.2014.0538.

187 As the authors of the study put it: Stefanie Johnson and David Hekman, " Women and Minorities Are Penalized for Promoting Diversity," *Harvard Business Review* (2016).

187 Google spent two years analyzing: Julia Rozovsky, "The Five Keys to a Successful Google Team," re:Work, November 17, 2015, https://rework .withgoogle.com/blog/five-keys-to-a-successful-google-team/.

189 Without a sponsor, will anyone: Hewlett and Green, "Black Women Ready to Lead."

189 There is also trepidation on the part of: Sylvia Ann Hewlett, Maggie Jackson, and Ellis Cose with Courtney Emerson, "Vaulting the Color Bar: How Sponsorship Levers Multicultural Professionals into Leadership," Center for Talent Innovation, 2012.

190 So how do you keep the constructive: Paola Cecchi-Dimeglio, "How Gender Bias Corrupts Performance Reviews, and What to Do About It," *Harvard Business Review*, April 12, 2017. See also: Caterina Kostoula, "How to Design Performance Reviews That Don't Fail Women," *Fast Company*, January 22, 2018, https://www.fastcompany.com/40518562/how-to-design -performance-reviews-that-dont-fail-women; Correll and Simard, "Research: Vague Feedback Is Holding Women Back"; David G. Smith, Judith E. Rosenstein, and Margaret C. Nikolov, "How Performance Evaluations Hurt Gender Equality," *Behavioral Scientist*, June 26, 2018, https://behavioralscientist .org/how-performance-evaluations-hurt-gender-equality/.

Chapter 11: Let Her Lead

195 Even when participants draw images: Heather Murphy, "Picture a Leader. Is She a Woman?" *New York Times*, March 16, 2018, https://www .nytimes.com/2018/03/16/health/women-leadership-workplace.html.

196 A woman focuses on the details: Herminia Ibarra and Otilia Obodaru, "Women and the Vision Thing," *Harvard Business Review*, January 2009.

199 "Women's likeability is something feminists use": Jessica Valenti, "She Who Dies with the Most 'Likes' Wins?" *Nation*, November 29, 2018, https://www.thenation.com/article/she-who-dies-most-likes-wins/.

199 In fact, recent research shows: Grainne Fitzsimons, Aaron Kay, and Jae Yun Kim, "'Lean In' Messages and the Illusion of Control," *Harvard Business Review*, July 30, 2018.

200 What stands out to me about much of the analysis: Michael Sokolove, "Follow Me," *New York Times Magazine*, February 5, 2006, https://www

.nytimes.com/2006/02/05/magazine/05coachk_96_101__116_117_.html
?pagewanted=all.

200 J. P. Morgan now has software: Hugh Son, "JPMorgan Software Does in Seconds What Took Lawyers 360,000 Hours," *Forbes*, February 27, 2017, https://www.bloomberg.com/news/articles/2017-02-28/jpmorgan-marshals -an-army-of-developers-to-automate-high-finance.

201 According to the report: Lee Rainie and Janna Anderson, "The Future of Jobs and Jobs Training," Pew Research Center, May 3, 2017, https:// www.pewinternet.org/2017/05/03/the-future-of-jobs-and-jobs-training/.

202 The process of becoming a leader: Herminia Ibarra, Robin J. Ely, and Deborah M. Kolb, "Women Rising: The Unseen Barriers," *Harvard Business Review*, September 2013, https://hbr.org/2013/09/women-rising-the-unseen -barriers.

202 Plus, women in top leadership roles sometimes: Martha Foschi, "Double Standards in the Evaluation of Men and Women," *Social Psychology Quarterly* 59 (1996): 237–54. See also Martha Foschi, "Double Standards for Competence: Theory and Research," *Annual Review of Sociology* 26 (2000): 21–42.

204 In testimony from former colleagues: Nellie Bowles and Liz Gannes, "Liveblog: As Ellen Pao Takes the Stand, the Test Now Is Likability," recode, March 9, 2015.

204 Howard Stern declared: Alex Williams, "Do We Really Hate Anne Hathaway?" *New York Times*, April 5, 2013.

204 During the 2008 presidential election: Transcript: The Democratic Debate in New Hampshire, *New York Times*, January 5, 2008, https://www .nytimes.com/2008/01/05/us/politics/05text-ddebate.html.

205 In a personal essay for *Lenny Letter*: Ellen Pao, "Silicon Valley Sexism IS Getting Better," *Lenny Letter*, November 11, 2015.

205 In an interview with *InStyle* magazine: Christopher Tennant, *InStyle*, September 2015.

Index

About the Author

Alicia Menendez is an MSNBC anchor and host of the *Latina to Latina* podcast. She has been dubbed "Ms. Millennial" by the *Washington Post*, "journalism's new gladiator" by *Elle*, and a "content queen" by *Marie Claire*; and her interviews and reporting have appeared on ABC News, Bustle, FusionTV, PBS, and Vice News. She lives in New Jersey with her husband and two daughters.